A
STUDY
OF
PRAYER

JOYCE CHURCH BRUNO

WESTBOW
PRESS®
A DIVISION OF THOMAS NELSON
& ZONDERVAN

WestBow Press books may be ordered through booksellers or by contacting:

WestBow Press
A Division of Thomas Nelson & Zondervan
1663 Liberty Drive
Bloomington, IN 47403
www.westbowpress.com
844-714-3454

Scripture quotations are taken from the Holy Bible, New International Version®, NIV®. Copyright © 1973, 1978, 1984 by Biblica, Inc.™ Used by permission of Zondervan. All rights reserved worldwide.

ISBN: 979-8-3850-2524-4 (sc)
ISBN: 979-8-3850-2526-8 (hc)
ISBN: 979-8-3850-2525-1 (e)

Library of Congress Control Number: 2024909617

Print information available on the last page.

WestBow Press rev. date: 05/08/2024

ACKNOWLEDGEMENTS

First and foremost, thank you to God Almighty who has gifted me with the talent to write, who has blessed me far more than I deserve, and who walks beside me each step of the way. I can't make it through a single second of a single day without You, heavenly Father, and I thank You for never leaving me. Through prayer, this book came to be; and without God, it wouldn't have been possible. It's been a long road, with many delays due to the pandemic and a busy lifestyle in general, but here it is at last! To God be the glory, now and forever! Amen! Without Him, I can do nothing!

To my husband, Rick, who has been my greatest supporter throughout life, through my creative writing endeavors, and throughout our marriage. I love you, honey, and I count you as one of my biggest blessings, and I thank God for you every day.

To my sister, Jan Hopkins-Campbell, who pushed me to get this study book published. Thank you for your constructive criticism and your input. Your support and encouragement have always meant so much to me. I'm proud that you are a published author yourself, I'm proud of your watercolor art business, and most of all, I'm proud to be your twin. Thank you for your love.

To Mike Kelley and Rodney Rochelle, our ministers at the Fairfield Church of Christ, who proofread my manuscript, made some comments and suggestions, and kept encouraging me to get this book published. I love you, brothers.

To Bill Hopkins, my father figure and mentor, thank you and Barb for taking me into your home while I was in nursing school and encouraging me in this work.

To the women of the Fairfield congregation, who let me teach this material so that I could get their feedback. You all have been sources of love and encouragement to me, and I love every one of you.

To Janine David, Leandra Drummy, and WestBow Press, thank you for believing in my book and for agreeing to publish it. It's been a long three-plus years since I started it, but the journey has been worth it!

CONTENTS

AN INTRODUCTION
TO PRAYER

Prayer is simply communication between man and a higher being. That definition makes prayer sound so simple when in fact it is more multidimensional, more awe-inspiring, more thought-provoking, and more purposeful. To understand the power available to us humans through the avenue of prayer, we must first decide how we view that "higher being"—in this case, God.

Do you see God as a loving Father who wants you to come to Him with all your fears, disappointments, and failures, or do you see Him as a tyrannical being ready to zap you into eternity if you mess up badly enough? How a person views his or her earthly father can frequently influence the way they view God, and as it was in my case, that may be unfortunate.

Growing up, my twin sister, older brother, and I all struggled with low self-esteem. In our home, we were never good enough, smart enough, attractive enough, athletic enough—in short, we were never enough. Both of our parents grew up with low self-esteem, and they perpetuated the cycle.

Around that same time, I came to view God as a higher being with a list of "dos" and "don'ts" that had to be checked off or avoided if I wanted to have any chance of making it to heaven. To me, He was that Supreme Being who wanted to zap me into eternity if I messed up badly enough. It wasn't until I was in my midthirties that I discovered that God wanted a *personal* relationship with me—*me!* And prayer? That took on an entirely new meaning too. I was "allowed" to talk to God about anything and everything.

Suddenly, prayer meant instant access to a father, albeit a heavenly Father who loved me, faults and all, and only wanted what was best for me. What an awesome thought! I had never experienced that in my entire life! And to think that the same God who created the universe by simply speaking it into existence, parted the Red Sea for the fleeing Israelite nation, calmed the storms on the Sea of Galilee, raised the dead, and did many other miracles too numerous to mention wanted to hear from *me!* What an awe-inspiring thought. The God who has created trillions and trillions of people even knew the number of hairs on my head! (Luke 12:7). I mattered to Someone!

Ephesians 3:12 tells us that "in him we have boldness and access in confidence through our faith in him." Because I am His child and because I have faith in Him, God loves me and wants to hear from me! That gives me the confidence to pray and ask Him for anything. Not that I expect to get everything I ask for, but just knowing that God is ready to listen makes all the difference.

Along this same line of thinking, do we, as Christians, realize the awesome power available to us through the avenue of prayer? Stop and think about this for a moment: Did Jesus ever reject one person who came to Him with a sincere request for help? How much more will God hear the sincere prayers of his obedient, repentant people? God has power over all evil, over all the world, over death. How many times do we use our prayers to tap into the power available to us? Do we not believe what the prophet Malachi said in chapter 3, verse 10, of his book when he wrote, "'Bring the whole tithe into the storehouse, that there may be food in my house, and test me now in this,' says Yahweh of Armies, 'if I will not open you the windows of heaven and pour you out a blessing, that there will not be room enough for?'" God is just waiting for us to communicate with Him, and He is ready to bless us with even more than we can ask or imagine.

In the book written by the apostle Paul in Ephesians 3:20–21, we also read, "Now to him who is able to do exceedingly abundantly above all that we ask or think, according to the power that works in us, to him be the glory in the assembly and in Christ Jesus to all generations forever and ever. Amen." We cannot even imagine the things God could do for us if we would just pray for His help, get out of His way, and allow Him to use us as He wills.

In his prayer in 2 Chronicles 20:5–12, King Jehoshaphat (who had allied himself with the evil King Ahab of Israel) conceded that only God could save the nation of Judah from its enemies. He acknowledged God's sovereign power and expressed his complete dependence upon God to save His people. Throughout the Bible, God led His people out of prisons, lions' dens, battles, catastrophes, and various trials. Because of this, we need to allow Him to lead us today.

Stop and think about this for a moment: people will always disappoint us. No human being will ever be able to fulfill all your emotional, mental, spiritual, or physical needs. It's human nature for all of us to think of ourselves first before thinking of others. It's natural for all of us to fall short of others' expectations. On the other hand, God is always waiting, ready to hear our deepest desires, ready to love us without judgment (unless we need it), ready to bless us. No one can love you to the same depth as God. No one.

Do you have someone in your life with whom you can be totally honest 100 percent of the time? Someone who knows *every single detail about you*—everything you have ever done, every thought you have ever had? Someone who knows every one of your deepest, darkest secrets? For most of us, the answer would be no. Although I truly love my husband of thirty-five years, to say that he unequivocally knows everything about me would be untrue. There always seems to be a part of me that I hold back and keep hidden for fear of rejection. God, on the other hand, knows everything about me and loves me anyway. He knows every thought I have ever had, every action I have ever done, and yet He still loves me.

Have you ever been brokenhearted and felt that none of your friends could even begin to understand the valley of your despair, how you struggled with a problem that seemed too personal to share even with your closest friend? Maybe like Job, your friends are not too good at comforting. (Heaven knows Job's three friends would never have won any awards for their empathy and compassion!) Yet God is concerned about everything we face, even if we bring difficult circumstances upon ourselves through our own human weaknesses and impulsivity. He alone can sort out the mess we have made of our lives. Whether what you are facing seems trivial or overwhelming, God wants you to bring it all to Him in prayer. Nothing you are facing is too small or too large to not bring to His attention.

How many of us struggle daily with some issues—addiction, overeating, poor health, loneliness, anxiety, financial difficulties, trying to raise godly children in an ungodly world—and turn to self-help books for our answers? Why don't we just turn to the One who has all the answers to life's problems—God Himself? When we are hurting the most, God does not avert His gaze, refusing to look into our tear-filled eyes. He sees the depths of our pain and longs to gather us close to Him. Why stress when you can pray to the one who spoke the universe into existence (Genesis 1:1), stopped the sun in the sky (Joshua 10:12), stopped the rain from falling to the earth for three years (1 Kings 17:1), made a donkey talk (Numbers 22:28), and raised His Son to eternal life (Luke 24:5–7)?

Prayer allows us to express our innermost thoughts to God (even though He already knows them) and allows us to open our hearts and minds to Him. If we pray and then wait and listen, He will answer us through circumstances, His Word, other people, or in a sudden peacefulness in our souls.

One of my earliest recollections of praying was when my twin sister and I were little. We shared bunk beds (she was usually in the top bunk, me usually in the bottom). Each night, we had a deal: we would say our nightly prayers and, when we were done, we would quietly knock on the headboard to let the other know that we were done praying so we could lie there and talk to each other. Many times though, my sister Jan would fall asleep during her prayers and I would lie waiting, waiting for the knock that wouldn't come. And inevitably, when I would say something and wake her up, she would shush me and tell me that she wasn't finished praying yet! We still laugh about this to this day! To be such an introverted preschooler, she was extremely long-winded when it came time for her nightly prayers!

Jan was also notorious for thanking God for *everything* when we were toddlers! She would thank God for Mommy and Daddy and brother Steve and me and all our pets and relatives and for birds and flowers and trees and grass … I'm sure you get the picture! In all fairness, though, to this day, she keeps a daily gratitude journal and lists things for which she is eternally grateful. She's even said that after a particularly rough day, the thing she may be most grateful for is that "this day is over," but at least she's thankful!

One of the greatest tragedies of life is that some people only pray to God in times of crisis. Otherwise, they choose to ignore God on a day-to-day basis. Our minister, Mike, calls these people "practical atheists." He describes them as "people who say that they believe in God, but don't live like He is a factor in their daily thinking or actions." To them, God is just there if they should need Him, but otherwise, they ignore Him until a crisis occurs. I still can't understand why people who don't want to spend any time with God in this life think that they will be spending eternity with God in heaven!

We all need to develop an intimate relationship with our heavenly Father, and you cannot become intimate with someone with whom you do not spend time. Think about when you were dating. Did you ever have a long-distance relationship? I did. It can be hard to get to know someone when you rarely spend time communicating. My husband and I had to schedule time to talk on the phone so that our relationship wouldn't fizzle. (This was before cell phones and texting, you see!) Likewise, we can come to know God more completely as we seek to communicate frequently and consistently with Him, opening our hearts to His presence and our minds to His answers to our prayers. We need to pray and study His Word consistently.

This study book is about prayer: why we should pray, why we don't pray as we should, what keeps God from hearing our prayers, how we should pray, and for whom we should pray and includes biblical examples of people who prayed, how God chose to answer their prayers, and what we can learn from them. The first chapter will deal specifically with the five types of prayers.

Before closing this introduction, I think it is pertinent that we should examine the purpose of prayer. Colossians 1:9–10 tells us, "For this cause, we also, since the day we heard this, don't cease praying and making requests for you, that you may be filled with the knowledge of his will in all spiritual wisdom and understanding, that you may walk worthily of the Lord, to please him in all respects, bearing fruit in every good work and increasing in the knowledge of God." One of the primary purposes of prayer is to seek the will of God, and whatever we do is to be done in the name of the Lord Jesus (see Colossians 3:17) and for His glory (1 Corinthians 10:31).

It seems like many people today are seeking fame, fortune, recognition, and admiration. Whether it's as the next TikTok sensation, the latest America's greatest ninja warrior, or the winner of the golden buzzer on *America's Got Talent*, they want to be known as someone famous. Scripture tells us that God is always to receive the glory for all we do. Do we, as Christians, pray about our situations, asking for them to bring glory to God?

I used to struggle with this too, especially when another nurse would be recognized at our hospital for the "exceptional care" she had given to a patient. I used to think, *What about me? I try to give exceptional care too!* Now I realize though, after listening to a comment that my twin sister made about God painting the pictures she makes and that she "merely held the paintbrush," that I too am merely an instrument in God's hands and He is to receive all the glory for anything I accomplish. (See 2 Thessalonians 1:11–12).

May God use this book to deepen your prayer life and strengthen your faith in our Lord Jesus Christ. To God be the glory forever and ever, amen.

LESSON 1

The Five Types of Prayers

THE FIRST TIME WE READ ABOUT PRAYER IN THE BIBLE IS IN GENESIS 4:26, which says, "At that time men began to call on Yahweh's name." To count the actual number of prayers in the Bible would be next to impossible, but the Bible does teach us that prayer was a vital part of life for many people who lived in lands plagued by wars, pestilence, hardships, and slavery. Page after page, chapter after chapter, book after book is filled with the prayers of God's people. From some of the earliest times, people seemed to recognize a higher being than themselves and prayed prayers of supplication to it.

To start our study of prayer, we must acknowledge that there are five different types of prayers; and in this chapter, we are going to examine each of them.

The first type is called prayers of supplication. Because by nature, humans are self-centered creatures, this is the easiest type of prayer to pray. These prayers are where we bring our requests before God and tell Him what we think we want or need. This kind of prayer is what many people think of when they consider the word *prayer*. Unfortunately, because it is the easiest type of prayer to pray, we must be careful that our prayer lives don't disintegrate into simply giving God a list of things we want. There are other types of prayers, and we must include them in our prayer lives as well.

Because prayers of supplication are when we bring our requests before God, they also include prayers asking for forgiveness for our sins. When we confess our sins before God and ask for forgiveness, God has promised to remove our sins and remember them no more. In 1 John 1:9, it says, "If we confess our sins, he is faithful and righteous to forgive us the sins, and to cleanse us from all unrighteousness." On a side note, we really need to be specific when we confess our sins, especially the ones we are keenly aware of. God knows every time we sin, and we need to ask for His forgiveness for specific times when we let Him down. Generalities won't do when it comes to the Lord. He wants us to acknowledge our specific sins, showing Him that we are aware of them too.

A prime example of a prayer of supplication in the Bible is when the apostles were trying to select a replacement for Judas Iscariot, who had betrayed the Lord and then killed himself (see Acts 1:24-26). What did the apostles do in this situation? Did they take a vote? Did they look to see who was the most popular of Jesus's followers? Did they organize a committee to study each man's qualifications and make recommendations? No, they prayed to God, who knew each man's heart and left the decision up to Him. After all, Jesus Himself prayed all night before selecting His twelve apostles (see Luke 6:12–16). The apostles were simply following the Lord's example.

When we are planning a project (for example, writing a book or planning a ladies' day), do we ask for God's blessing on it? Do we seek God's direction? Do we ask Him to reveal His will? Notice how Nehemiah prayed to God before he approached King Artaxerxes about going to Jerusalem to rebuild the wall of Jerusalem (Nehemiah 2:4). We too need to ask for God's blessings on our plans and projects before we begin them and as we work on them. This book you are holding has come about through many prayers to God, and to Him be the glory!

Sometimes we get so hung up on praying for what we want or think we need that we overlook other things for which we should be praying. For example, how often do we pray for boldness to proclaim God's Word to a lost world? For many of us, this would mean stepping out of our comfort zones, and we don't like doing this. But this is exactly what God calls us to do in His Great Commission (Matthew 28:19–20). One thing we need to remember when it comes to evangelism is that God calls us to share the Gospel, but He does not make us responsible for the outcome.

And do we ever think to pray as David did in Psalm 139:23–24 that God would search our hearts and show us if there is anything offensive (to Him) in us? Or are we afraid of what God might find in our hearts?

Honestly, I have never prayed this prayer before. However, after working on this book, I have decided that I need to add this type of prayer to my prayer life so that God can help me be more Christlike. There may be things that I have unknowingly done that offend God, and if so, I want Him to point them out to me so that I may ask for His forgiveness and try to never do them again.

On a side note, my mother used to tell me, "Be careful what you pray for because you just might get it!" And it's true. If you pray for patience, God may send difficult situations or people into your life to test you. If you pray for wisdom, God may send puzzling circumstances your way. Prayers for unselfishness may require lessons in giving to those less fortunate, perhaps through a natural disaster that hits some other part of the world. We pray for more faith and are suddenly confronted with our own mortality when we are given a terminal diagnosis. We pray that this nation will turn back to God, but think about it: when has it done so in the past? During the two world wars? After September 11, 2001? Do we realize that it might take a catastrophe to turn the United States back to God? Are we prepared for this?

The second type of prayer is called intercessory prayer. This is where we pray on behalf of other people. The Bible is full of intercessory prayers. Many times, in the Old Testament, intercessory prayers were offered during wars for people's lives to be spared (see 2 Chronicles 20:5–19) or when God was about to take vengeance on a city for the inhabitants' wickedness (see Genesis 18:23–33). Intercessory prayers in the New Testament were often offered for the spiritual well-being of an individual (see Luke 22:31–32) or for the healing of an individual (see Acts 9:36–43).

The greatest intercessory prayer was prayed by Jesus Himself in the seventeenth chapter of the book of John. In the first five verses, Jesus prays for Himself. In verses 6–19, Jesus prays for His disciples. In verses 20–26, Jesus prays for all believers, including those who will follow Him in the future. Imagine! Jesus was praying for you before you were even born!

Although both Abraham and Moses spoke directly with God, they still interceded on behalf of others when God threatened to destroy the cities of Sodom and Gomorrah in Genesis 18:16–32 and when He threatened to destroy the Israelite nation for their sinfulness in Exodus 32:9–14 and verses30–32 of the same chapter. These are only two examples of the many times one of God's people interceded on behalf of others.

The Bible even tells us that the Holy Spirit intercedes for us. In Romans 8:26, we read, "In the same way, the Spirit also helps our weaknesses, for we don't know how to pray as we ought. But the Spirit himself makes intercession for us with groaning which cannot be uttered." Have you ever been so overwhelmed with a situation, not even knowing what's the best thing for which to pray that you felt like throwing up your hands and saying, "Lord Jesus, please just take control because I don't even know what to pray for anymore?" That's OK. In those situations, the Holy Spirit knows our hearts and can convey to God what we don't even know how to say ourselves. And He does, and God understands. Isn't it comforting to know that even when we get tongue-tied or overwhelmed, the Holy Spirit and God understand and continue to help us?

Romans 8:34 tells us that Jesus also intercedes for us. In this passage, we read, "Who is he who condemns? It is Christ who died, yes rather, who was raised from the dead, who is at the right hand of God, who also makes intercession for us."

In the New Testament, in the book of Acts, we read of a group of believers who prayed for the apostles Peter and John. When both men were brought before the elders and teachers of the law in Jerusalem, what was it that enabled them to be bold in proclaiming the death and resurrection of Jesus Christ despite just having been put into prison? Besides their personal faith, it was the prayers of the believers in the first-century church. After Peter and John had been released from prison, their own people continued to pray for them to have boldness in proclaiming the good news (Acts 4:1–29).

Jesus prayed an intercessory prayer for Peter in Luke 22:31–32. These verses say, "The Lord said, 'Simon, Simon, behold, Satan asked to have all of you that he might sift you as wheat, but I prayed for you, that your faith wouldn't fail. You, when once you have turned again, establish your brothers.'" Can you imagine having the Lord Himself praying for you? I certainly think that that would have bolstered the apostle Peter's faith!

Jesus even prayed an intercessory prayer while on the cross for those who were crucifying Him (Luke 23:34). Yes, Jesus's last recorded words were a prayer for others, asking God to forgive them because they had no idea Who it was that they were crucifying.

We too can pray intercessory prayers for others—those who are sick or have lost loved ones, those who are struggling through difficult financial situations, and those who are wrestling with family issues or problems at work. Have you ever struggled with the problem of how to help a friend who is burdened with ill health, the consequences of poor choices made in his or her lifetime, addiction, homelessness, or some other crisis? In these cases (and many others), you may feel that the only thing you can do for your friend is pray—and that's exactly what God wants you to do! Bring your friend's name before the throne of God and watch Him work in ways that you, in your human frailty, never could. The true test of faith is when you trust God enough to turn over to Him a person or situation that matters a great deal to you.

For example, do we pray for our spouses? Do we pray for our children and grandchildren? Do we pray while they are still young that they will find a godly mate who will love and support them through this life on the road to heaven? Do we pray for their friends? Do we, like Job, pray for the forgiveness of their sins? (Job 1:5). Being a child today is difficult at best (I wouldn't want to do my childhood all over again!), and children need all the prayers we can give them!

The third type of prayer is one of thanksgiving. This is when we acknowledge what God has done or is going to do for us. One of the longest prayers of thanksgiving recorded in the Bible is in 1 Kings 8:12–61, in which Solomon prayed at the dedication of the Lord's temple.

In John 6:11, Jesus thanked God for material blessings. In John 11:41–44, Jesus thanked God *before* He raised Lazarus from the dead. Do we ever thank God in advance for His answers to our prayers, believing that He *will* answer them? Do we ever get so caught up with providing God with a list of our wants and needs that we forget to thank Him for the blessings He has already provided? Ingratitude is a sin, and each one of us must guard against it. Every day, we should pray a prayer of thanksgiving to Almighty God for all the blessings He has already given us! Every day we are alive is a gift from God.

After God had answered Daniel's prayer by telling him what King Nebuchadnezzar had dreamed, Daniel took a few minutes to thank God for His faithfulness before rushing off to see Arioch, the man who was assigned the task of executing the wise men of Babylon (see Daniel 2:1–24, especially 19–23). Notice in this story that Daniel thanked God for the ability to interpret the dream. Do we take the time to thank God for answered prayers? Do we give God the credit for the talents to accomplish various things in our lifetimes? Do we acknowledge how much God does for us on a daily basis?

First Thessalonians 5:16–18 says, "Always rejoice. Pray without ceasing. In everything give thanks, for this is the will of God in Christ Jesus toward you." It's easy to thank God when things are going well in our lives, but when we face trials, can we still say that God is good and worthy of our praise?

My husband and I once tried to adopt a baby because I had to have a hysterectomy before we were married due to stage 4 endometriosis. Maggie was our fourth attempt at adoption and the closest we ever got to having a child of our own. But after having her for almost a year, her birth mother changed her mind about the adoption and we had to give her back. The night before we were to return her, we had a mini prayer service at church for anyone who wanted to come and pray for Maggie before she went back to her birth mother and a less-than-ideal home life situation. One of the songs I had selected for the service was "God Is So Good."

At that time, a very close friend who was also devastated by what was happening became upset with me for selecting this song. Her response was, "I can't sing that song now. I don't believe it in this situation."

But as I reminded my friend, "In the words of Job, 'Shall we receive good at the hands of God, and shall we not receive evil?' God is good all the time" (Job 2:10). Did that mean that I didn't find these circumstances just as devastating as my friend did? No, of course not. For three years afterward, I could barely function after losing Maggie. I even found it difficult to get out of bed. I no longer smiled or laughed.

But as a grief counselor told me, "You will grieve for her like she died because Maggie Bruno no longer exists. She went back to a different life and a different name." My husband, my family and friends, and I did grieve for her as she had died. But I still trusted God and His infinite wisdom. After three years, I felt the cloud over me lift and realized that my life *would* go on. (I will share more later in this book on how God used this heartbreaking situation to show His love for me, my husband, and everyone who grieved the loss of Maggie.)

The fourth type of prayer is prayers of relinquishment. These are prayers when we ask God for what we would like to happen but offer to give up our will for His. These are probably the hardest prayers to pray. A perfect example of this type of prayer is when Jesus was praying in the garden of Gethsemane. In Matthew 26:39, we see Jesus praying the following words: "My Father, if it is possible, let this cup pass away from me; nevertheless, not what I desire, but what you desire."

The apostle Paul is another example of someone who prayed a prayer of relinquishment, giving up his will for God's will. In 2 Corinthians 12:7, Paul tells his readers that he was "given a thorn in the flesh." The scripture does not tell us what Paul's "thorn" was, but in verses 7–10, we learn that Paul prayed three times for it to be removed. These were not just simple casual prayers, but deep heartfelt prayers of anguish. I don't think that this *thorn* was simply a mere irritation, but a life-changing, challenging-to-deal-with health condition. Otherwise, Paul wouldn't have been so persistent in wanting to be rid of it. Paul hardly struck me as a wimp, yet he asked for the removal of this thorn three times. The great apostle, who had survived shipwrecks, beatings, stoning, and snake bites, didn't want this thorn in his life. Paul finally concludes this passage in 2 Corinthians 12, however, by saying in verse 9, "He has said to me, 'My grace is sufficient for you, for my power is made perfect in weakness.'" Paul goes on to say in verses 9–10, "Most gladly therefore I will rather glory in my weaknesses, that the power of Christ may rest on me. Therefore I take pleasure in weaknesses, in injuries, in necessities, in persecutions and in distresses, for Christ's sake. For when I am weak, then I am strong." Paul learned to accept God's will and be content even if it meant that he would have to deal with this thorn for the remainder of his life.

The last type of prayer, and maybe the one we pray the second least, is prayers of adoration and praise. How often do we show our reverence and respect for who God is when we pray to Him? Do we acknowledge Him as Creator of the universe, Lord of our lives, and Savior of all who do His will?

The easiest way to pray prayers of adoration or praise is like what one of the men of our small congregation recently did: pray the scriptures. Many examples of beautiful scriptures to pray can be found in the book of Psalms (see Psalm 8; Psalm18:1–3; and Psalm 145 for just a few examples). God loves to hear us pray scripture! We need to do this more often than we do! It is a great way to pray prayers of praise and reverence to God.

THOUGHT QUESTIONS

1. Do you believe that you should be careful about what you pray? Why or why not?

2. Do you find it hard to remember to thank God for what He has already done for you? Have you ever thanked Him in advance for His answer *before* He gave it to you?

3. Which type of prayer do you find yourself gravitating toward the most? Which types of prayer do you find it difficult to pray? How can you incorporate these other types of prayers into your daily prayer life?

4. Do you ever feel that your prayer life has disintegrated into simply a list of what you want God to do for you? How can you change that?

5. Do you pray for your spouse, your children, and your grandchildren and their friends? Do you find it easy or hard to pray for others?

6. Have you ever struggled with a difficult situation and didn't even know for what you should pray? What did you do in that situation?

LESSON 2

Why Should We Pray?

IMAGINE THAT A WOMAN WANTS A MOTHER'S RING FOR MOTHER'S DAY one year but never thinks to mention this to her family. How likely is it that she will get it? Suppose a young man, who is dying of terminal cancer, wants to be an organ donor or donate his body to medical science but never discusses this with his parents. How likely is it that this will happen if he doesn't tell them? God wants us to tell Him (in prayer) what is important to us—our joys and sorrows, our fears and desires. Prayer is the only real way to communicate with God as noted in the introduction to this book.

Someone once asked, "But if God knows everything, why should I pray? Doesn't the Bible say that God already knows what I need before I ask?" That is very true, and that passage is found in Matthew 6:8, which says, "Therefore don't be like them (the hypocrites) for your Father knows what things you need, before you ask him." In that case, if God already knows what we need, why should we even pray?

For one thing, we are commanded in the scriptures to pray. Romans 12:12 says, "Rejoicing in hope, enduring in troubles; continuing steadfastly in prayer." Prayer is not to be an occasional occurrence but a daily activity. We are also to make a commitment to persevere in prayer.

Colossians 4:2 (NIV) reads, "Devote yourselves to prayer, being watchful and thankful." Devoting ourselves to prayer implies a disciplined practice that makes this activity of the utmost importance to us. Devoted means that we are willing to put forth a great effort to do or accomplish something. We are not just to have a prayer list. We are to have a prayerful life!

9

We are also commanded in this verse to be thankful and watchful. Being watchful could mean guarding against distractions or hindrances that may interrupt your prayer life. What do you think it means?

In 1 Thessalonians 5:17, we read, "Pray without ceasing." This doesn't mean that you should pray every minute of every day, which would be next to impossible, but prayer should be an integral part of your everyday life. There are prayers called "sentence prayers," generally only one or two sentences long, which a person can pray throughout the day as they come to mind—maybe thankfulness for kindness shown or a specific prayer for someone with whom we have had a chance encounter.

Ephesians 6:18 says, "With all prayer and requests, praying at all times in the Spirit." "All prayers and requests" imply that nothing is off-limits to pray, but in later chapters of this study guide, we will learn why God might not hear our prayers or why He might say no to our prayers. Still, we shouldn't hesitate to bring *everything* to God in prayer. This verse tells us that we must also pray always in the Spirit. Remember, praying in the Spirit enables the Spirit to intercede for us when we are unable to say what is on our hearts.

Other passages that command us to pray include Matthew 7:7–8, Luke 11:9–10, 1 Timothy 2:1, and Matthew 5:44.

Jesus Himself also set an example for us to follow. In Luke 5:16, we read, "But he withdrew himself into the desert, and prayed." The Bible tells us that Jesus often withdrew by Himself to spend time with and get guidance from God. Being alone with God allows us to pray without distractions. Just like Jesus, we all need to spend quality time alone with our heavenly Father. God wants that kind of uninterrupted communication with us, and we need that uninterrupted time with God.

Jesus obviously prayed in public on many occasions. One such occasion is found in Matthew 11:25, which says, "At that time Jesus answered, 'I thank you, Father, Lord of heaven and earth, that you hid these things from the wise and understanding, and revealed them to infants.'" Jesus spoke these words after John the Baptist sent some of his followers to Jesus to see if He was the promised Messiah or if they were to look for another. By saying this, Jesus showed that He knew that the teachers of the law and the wise men of the day would reject Him, but that it would be the lowly, uneducated people who would welcome Him into their lives.

Jesus prayed before meals as we read in Matthew 26:26, which says, "As they were eating, Jesus took bread, gave thanks for it, and broke it. He gave it to the disciples and said, 'Take, eat; this is my body.'" We too should be thankful for both of our daily bread and the Lord's Supper, which we partake of to honor and remember Jesus's sacrifice on the cross for each of us.

Jesus also prayed before making important decisions, as in Luke 6:12–13, which says, "In these days, he went out to the mountain to pray, and he continued all night in prayer to God. When it was day, he called his disciples, and from them he chose twelve, whom he also named apostles." We need to follow Jesus's example by giving thanks for our food and other material and spiritual blessings and to pray for God's guidance when we must make important decisions. If we pray for spiritual wisdom when faced with a decision, God will provide it.

Sometimes our daily lives become nothing more than a struggle. As a nurse at the local hospital in the emergency room, I am witness to all kinds of suffering and sorrow. Rarely do we see anyone on the best day of his or her life. Most of the time we see people struggling with the death of a loved one, serious injuries and pain, addiction, heartache, anxiety, and depression. At times, it can become overwhelming. My recent prayers have become, "Lord, I honestly cannot make it through a single minute of a single day without you." All of us need to recognize and acknowledge our utter dependence upon God for everything we have and everything we are. I honestly don't know how anyone can make it through a single day without the Lord!

Matthew 6:6 reads as follows: "But you, *when you pray*, enter into your inner room, and having shut your door, pray to your Father who is in secret, and your Father who sees in secret will reward you openly" (emphasis added). Notice that Jesus said, "*when* you pray," not "*if* you pray." Prayer is expected of all believers. Our personal prayers are to be between us and God. We are to find time to pray to God privately, quietly, and reverently.

Jesus exhorts us in Matthew 6:5–8, "When you pray, you shall not be as the hypocrites, for they love to stand and pray in the synagogues and in the corners of the streets, that they may be seen by men. Most certainly, I tell you, they have received their reward. But when you pray, enter into your inner room, and having shut your door, pray to your Father who is in secret, and your Father who sees in secret will reward you openly. In praying, don't use vain repetitions, as the Gentiles do: for they think they will be heard for their much speaking. Therefore, don't be like them, for your Father knows what things you need, before you ask Him." Jesus tells us that God wants our prayers to be personal time between us and Him, and if we pray in secret, He will reward us. But if we pray long-winded, overly pious prayers, trying to impress others with our big words and posturing, God says the praise of men will be our reward. So which would you rather have: man's approval or God's?

Are there any personal benefits we can derive from prayer? First, the Bible tells us that prayer is good for our emotional well-being. Philippians 4:6–7 tells us, "In nothing be anxious, but in everything by prayer and petition with thanksgiving, let your requests be made known to God. And the peace of God, which surpasses all understanding, will guard your hearts and thoughts in Christ Jesus." When you are anxious and you turn your struggles over to God in prayer, you will find a peace that only God can provide, a peace that surpasses even our understanding.

First Peter 5:7 says, "Casting all your worries on him, because he cares for you." Notice that this verse doesn't say to bring a few select problems to God, but instead, we can bring *everything* to our Lord because he cares for us. Giving our concerns to God can relieve our anxiety because we no longer must be the ones to work out the solution. A great deal of our daily stress comes from carrying around and worrying about things over which we personally have no control. This can lead to many mental and physical ailments. I see examples of this every day working in our local hospital's emergency department. People struggle with worry and anxiety over issues that they cannot control. Many times I have prayed for God's peace to envelope one who was anxious, depressed, or worried.

Jacob prayed for peace of mind when he was afraid to face his brother, Esau, after he had stolen his older brother's birthright twenty years earlier (Genesis 32:9–12). Jacob needn't have worried though because Genesis 33:4 says, "Esau ran to meet him, embraced him, fell on his neck, kissed him, and they wept." God can take a situation that we feel is hopeless and change it for the better. All we must do is pray and trust Him. Can you imagine how relieved Jacob was when Esau hugged him and forgave him for the wrong he had done to him? Do you realize that Jacob probably carried around the guilt and anxiety over his own sinful actions for twenty years? What a long time to carry such a burden!

Prayer can change our outlook on life and our circumstances as it did for Hannah in 1 Samuel 1:1–18. Hannah was inconsolable and despondent when she first entered the temple with her husband, desperately wanting a child but unable to get pregnant; but after praying to God and speaking to the priest Eli, her heart was lighter and her countenance improved. Prayer changes the one who prays, but God never changes, and that is comforting. For the first time in years, Hannah probably felt that God had finally heard her prayers, and she was able to go home and rest in the assurances of Eli.

In another example of this, we read in Acts 12 that Peter was in prison and the church members were earnestly praying for his release. God heard their prayers and sent His angel to free Peter from prison. When Peter realized that he was free, he went to the house of Mary, the mother of John Mark, and knocked on the door. A servant girl named Rhoda saw Peter at the door and ran inside to announce his presence to the others who were gathered there, but no one believed her. Peter had to keep knocking until someone would come and let him in! Like these believers, we can't just pray for God to do great things in our lives. We must pray with the expectation that He *will* do great things in our lives! After all, you shouldn't go to a prayer meeting and pray for rain if you're not going to bring an umbrella!

Prayer and spending time with Jesus in His Word take away fear. Acts 4:13 tells us, "Now when they saw the boldness of Peter and John, and perceived that they were unlearned and ignorant men, they marveled." Peter and John didn't have degrees in the Bible or theology. They were not professional orators or lecturers. They were rough, uneducated fishermen. Only God could have given them the eloquence and boldness to preach His word, and the rulers, elders, and teachers of the law realized this and were amazed.

The 107th Psalm has an interesting story within it. Verses 23–30 say, "Those who go down to the sea in ships, who do business in great waters. These see Yahweh's deeds, and his wonders in the deep. For he commands, and raises the stormy wind, which lifts up its waves. They mount up to the sky; they go down again to the depths. Their soul melts away because of trouble. They reel back and forth, and stagger like a drunken man, *and are at their wits' end* (emphasis mine). Then they cry to Yahweh in their trouble, and he brings them out of their distress. He makes the storm a calm, so that its waves are still. Then they are glad because it is calm so he brings them to their desired haven." Think about it: like these sailors, when we are at our wits' end, when we don't know where to go or what to do, we can go to God and He will help us—even if the circumstances in which we find ourselves is one of our own making. What a relief it is to be able to pray to God and say, "Well, Father, I did it again. I goofed up big-time, and I need Your help to straighten out this mess that I have gotten myself into," and know that like the loving Father He is, He will help us. On the other hand, though, we need to remember that we cannot deliberately sin and expect God to bail us out of our mess. We still must suffer the consequences of our actions because God will not automatically take those away, and we need to strive not to make the same mistakes again.

There are certain things in life that can only be accomplished by the power of God and can only be accessed through the power of prayer. Mark 9:17– 29 tells of a time when the disciples were unable to cast a demon out of a young man. Verse 28 says, "When he (Jesus) had come into the house, his disciples asked him privately, 'Why couldn't we cast it out?'" And in verse 29, it says, "He said to them, 'This kind can come out by nothing, except by prayer and fasting.'" This situation shows that there are certain circumstances when only God can prevail. It's not up to us with our money and our fancy degrees and our material wealth and scientific knowledge, but only God can change certain situations. It really annoys me when doctors say of a terminally ill person, "Well, he's in God's hands now." Excuse me! He's *always* been in God's hands! Doctors and nurses are just instruments in the hands of God. God has the ultimate power to affect the outcome.

Prayer united the believers in the first-century church. Acts 2:42 says, "They continued steadfastly in the apostles' teaching and fellowship, in the breaking of bread, and prayer." Prayer and fellowship were daily occurrences for early Christians, and both unified the church. It would be difficult to remain standoffish with others when you are eating and praying with them daily.

The Bible tells us that God is near us when we pray. What inspiring words we read in Deuteronomy 4:5– 9, which say, "See, I have taught you decrees and laws as the Lord my God commanded me, so that you may follow them in the land you are entering to take possession of it. Observe them carefully, for this will show your wisdom and understanding to the nations, who will hear about all these decrees and say, 'Surely this great nation is a wise and understanding people.' What other nation is so great as to have their gods near them the way the Lord our God is near us whenever we pray to him? And what other nation is so great as to have such righteous decrees and laws as the body of laws I am setting before you today? Only be careful, and watch yourselves closely so that you do not forget the things your eyes have seen or let them slip from your heart as long as you live. Teach them to your children and to their children after them." If this was the only reason to pray, it would be enough: *God is near us when we pray.* What better reason to pray is there than this?

The Bible also teaches us that prayer gives us power over evil. In Matthew 26:41, Jesus tells his apostle Peter, "Watch and pray, that you don't enter into temptation. The spirit indeed is willing but the flesh is weak." Jesus knew that Peter, the impetuous natural-born leader of the apostles, was going to face his own trials soon. As a result, Jesus urged Peter to pray to God for strength to stand against the devil and his temptations. I don't understand people who think that they can stand up to the devil without God. None of us are that strong on our own!

When you pray to God, you are acknowledging that you are not God and that you are not in control of your situation. After all, if you could work out every solution to every problem you encounter, you wouldn't need God, right? Prayers show our dependence upon God for everything. If we could handle every situation that came up, there wouldn't be any need for us to pray, would there? Scripture tells us, "Let's therefore draw near with boldness to the throne of grace, that we may receive mercy and may find grace for help in time of need" (Hebrews 4:16). Who else but Jesus makes this kind of promise of help? We don't have to be afraid to approach our heavenly Father because, like a father, He only wants what is best for us. God wants to help us, but we have to allow Him to do it His way, in His timing.

Another key verse in the Bible that emphasizes our dependency upon God is found in the Gospel of John 15:5, which says, "I am the vine. You are the branches. He who remains in me and I in him bears much fruit, for apart from me you can do nothing." I read passages like this and wonder how on earth people can try to live their lives without God! The Bible plainly says that apart from God, you can do nothing. Why would we even try? But we do and then wonder why we fall flat on our faces. So many of our struggles would be lessened if we would just depend on God for everything the way He wants us to!

It pleases God when we ask Him for spiritual wisdom to discern His will for our lives. James 1:5 says, "But if any of you lacks wisdom, let him ask of God, who gives to all liberally and without reproach, and it will be given to him." (This is not just worldly wisdom, but godly wisdom. We will examine the difference in more depth in a later chapter.)

Prayer also brings glory to God and allows His power to be seen. Have you ever prayed for someone who was critically ill or injured and then, against all odds, they pulled through and survived? There was a young lady in our community who was involved in a terrible gun accident several years ago and given only a 1 percent chance of survival by the doctors at Vanderbilt University Medical Center in Nashville. It seemed like everyone in the community was praying for her; and not only did she survive, but she is also now beautiful, healthy, and thriving. It was obvious that God had a hand in her recovery and that He had big plans for her life. She is a walking testimony to what God can do. To God be the glory!

Jesus said in John 14:13, "Whatever you will ask in my name, I will do it, that the Father may be glorified in the Son." The phrase "in my name" implies that there are specific conditions to receiving affirmative answers to our prayers, and we will examine these in depth in a later chapter. But everything we do must bring glory to God, including the things for which we pray. First Corinthians 10:31 reminds us, "Whether therefore you eat, or drink, *or whatever you do, do all to the glory of God*" (emphasis mine). Do you realize that even the smallest thing you do can bring glory to God?

When Jesus raised His friend Lazarus from the dead, the Bible tells us in John 11:41–42, "So they took away the stone from the place where the dead man was lying. Jesus lifted up his eyes, and said, 'Father, I thank you that you listened to me. I know that you always listen to me, but because of the multitude standing around I said this, that they may believe that you sent me.'" Jesus simply prayed to emphasize a point to those standing there, that God is always available and always ready to listen to us when we pray to Him. Jesus knew when He traveled to Bethany that Lazarus would already be dead and that He was going to raise him to life as a testimony to His disciples as to who He was, the powerful Son of God, who had power over life and death. He deliberately prayed to God so that His disciples would recognize from where His power came.

Isaiah even tells us in Isaiah 65:24, "It will happen that, before they call, I will answer; and while they are yet speaking, I will hear." God can answer our prayers before we even finish praying them. He already knows what we need. He just wants to hear it from us.

THOUGHT QUESTIONS

1. What are some reasons we should pray? What are some benefits of praying?

2. Members of the first-century church devoted themselves to daily prayer. Do you think that we (individually and collectively as a church) pray enough today? Why or why not?

3. Do you think daily personal prayer time is important? Do you pray daily? Do you have a special place set aside where you go to pray without distractions?

4. In the book of Daniel 6:1–23, we learn that Daniel led a disciplined prayer life. Despite the fact that King Darius had issued an edict that any man praying to anyone besides the king within the next thirty days would be thrown into the lions' den, Daniel continued praying to the God of heaven. If you had been Daniel, could you have continued praying to God, knowing what the potential consequences were? What if the United States outlawed prayer or religious gatherings? Would you continue to pray and go to church, knowing that you might be imprisoned for breaking the law? What do you think it takes to develop a faith like Daniel's?

LESSON 3

Why Don't We Pray Like We Should?

THE BIBLE TEACHES US IN MATTHEW 7:7–8, "ASK, AND IT WILL BE GIVEN you. Seek, and you will find. Knock, and it will be opened to for you. For everyone who asks receives. He who seeks finds. To him who knocks it will be opened." This is a promise from God, and we need to claim it.

On the other hand, notice that *we* must initiate this promise. We must "ask, seek, and knock." God is not going to search us out or force us to get us to do these things. It all goes back to our *free will*.

Perhaps we are ashamed to ask something of God. Maybe we think that He will get tired of hearing from us. Or what if what we're asking for isn't big enough in the whole grand scheme of the universe? Why would God condescend low enough to grant our puny request? Who are we to ask something of almighty God?

Another biblical promise is found in Malachi 3:10, which says, "'Bring the whole tithe into the storehouse, that there may be food in my house, and test me now in this,' says Yahweh of Armies, 'if I will open you the windows of heaven, and pour you out a blessing, that there will not be room enough for.'" Again, do we realize the awesome power available to us through the avenue of prayer? Do we realize that God is just waiting to bless us and bless us more abundantly than we can even imagine? Can you imagine a blessing that even God says "there will not be room enough for?" That sounds like a pretty awesome blessing to me!

Since this is what scripture teaches us, why don't we live like we believe these promises? Why don't we ask God for what we want and believe that He will answer our prayers? What holds us back?

First, some of us don't pray because we don't really believe that God can or will answer our prayers, or maybe we doubt that He even cares for us. After all, we are but one individual in a world that has played host to billions and billions of people! But Matthew tells us in his Gospel in Matthew 10:29–31, "Aren't two sparrows sold for an assarion coin? Not one of them falls on the ground apart from your Father's will, but the very hairs of your head are all numbered. Therefore, don't be afraid. You are of more value than many sparrows." Can you imagine that of all the people who have ever lived, God knows you so intimately that He knows how many hairs are on your head? I don't think this is simply a figure of speech; I believe that we can take this promise literally. God knows how many hairs are on our heads. God knows each one of us intimately. After all, He created us. Why wouldn't He?

Another promise that God has made to His people is found in Jeremiah 29:11–13, which says, "'For I know the thoughts that I think toward you,' says Yahweh, 'thoughts of peace and not of evil, to give you hope and a future. You shall call on me, and you shall go and pray to me, and I will listen to you. You shall seek me and find me, when you search for me with all your heart.'" Now, granted, at that time God was speaking to the remnant of the remaining Israelites living in exile, but doesn't it stand to reason that God loves His children just as much today? Don't you think God also has hope and a future waiting for His children today if they are willing to trust Him?

Do you believe that you have a specific purpose for being alive at this time in history? Did you ever wonder why you were born when you were instead of, say, during the Dark Ages or the Civil War or sometime in the future? Maybe one of your children will become president one day and lead this great country. Perhaps God put you on earth to lead someone to Him. Could it be that God wants you to write a book or a piece of music for Him? Or maybe He just wants you to live your best life possible for Him in your own little corner of the world. Each of us has a purpose, and each of our lives touches others. We all need to live our best lives possible for God.

The great patriarch Moses was one eyewitness to the awesome power of God. We read in Exodus 14:21–22, "Moses stretched out his hand over the sea, and Yahweh caused the sea to go back by a strong east wind all night, and made the sea dry land, and the waters were divided. The children of Israel went into the middle of the sea on the dry ground, and the waters were a wall to them on their right hand, and on their left." And yet although Moses had seen God hold back the waters of the Red Sea, later, he had the audacity to doubt whether the Lord God Almighty could care for His people in the wilderness! In Numbers 11:18–23, we read, "Tell the people: 'Consecrate yourselves in preparation for tomorrow, when you will eat meat. The Lord heard you when you wailed, "If only we had meat to eat! We were better off in Egypt!" Now the Lord will give you meat, and you will eat it. You will not eat it for just one day, or two days, or five, ten or twenty days, but for a whole month—until it comes out your nostrils and you loathe it—because you have rejected the Lord, who is among you, and have wailed before him, saying, "Why did we ever leave Egypt?"'" But Moses said, "Here I am among six hundred thousand men on foot, and you say, 'I will give them meat to eat for a whole month!' Would they have enough if flocks and herds were slaughtered for them? Would they have enough if all the fish in the sea were caught for them?'" The Lord answered Moses, "Is the Lord's arm too short? Now you will see whether or not what I say will come true for you."

This is also a perfect example of someone (the people of Israel) who prayed for something they thought they wanted, but because they did not wait to see what else God might provide for them, they ended up receiving meat every day until they were heartily sick of it! There are two very important lessons for us here: sometimes what we think we want is not what we really want, and maybe God has something even better in mind for us if we will just shut up and let Him handle the situation in His own way! Sometimes when you pester God enough, He will give you what you think you want, even if it is not something in your best interest. We need to be careful to ask for what we really want and really want what we ask for.

How many times do we see how God has taken care of us in the past, and yet we continue to doubt His ability to care for our needs in the future? We find it easy to criticize Moses, but are we any better? Don't we doubt God's ability to care for us just as much as Moses did? We need to reflect frequently on how God has taken care of us in the past in to strengthen our hearts for future trials.

Why don't we claim biblical promises such as Ephesians 3:20–21, which say, "Now to him who is able to do exceedingly abundantly above all that we ask or think, according to the power that works in us, to him be the glory in the assembly and in Christ Jesus to all generations forever and ever. Amen?" God is all-powerful, all-knowing, omnipresent, and yet we continue to doubt His abilities and promises. Imagine: God can do even more than we ask or imagine! I don't know about you, but I have a hefty imagination, so it's a blessing to know that God can even exceed my anticipations. We can't even envision what God could do in our lives if we would just get out of the way and let Him!

Maybe God hasn't answered our previous prayers the way we wanted and we are disappointed in Him. Maybe we just can't wrap our minds around why God allowed our loved one to die or why that relationship we struggled to maintain failed. I read someone's post on Facebook once that said, "I can't pray to God because He allows babies to die." To me, that person thinks that God doesn't care or doesn't have any clue why He does what He does. But I believe that God has a plan for everything, even if we don't understand it.

OK, so what if we could know the "why" a disaster happened? Would it really make it any easier to bear? Would it lessen our grief? Ease our heartache? One thing we need to remember is an admonition found in Isaiah 55:8–9, which says, "'For my thoughts are not your thoughts, and your ways are not my ways,' says Yahweh. 'For as the heavens are higher than the earth, so are my ways higher than your ways, and my thoughts than your thoughts.'" If we were to understand the *why* of every difficult situation that comes our way, what becomes of faith? Faith is not understanding the why but believing anyway.

I took care of an elderly woman once, who had immigrated here from another country. She had lost her daughter and her husband over time, and then she had been given a terminal diagnosis herself. When I asked if I could include her in my personal prayers, she said to me, "Save your personal prayers for yourself. I don't believe in God. I did at one time, in the old country. But then He took my husband and my daughter, and I quit believing." How sad that this woman had allowed circumstances to rob her of her faith and peace in God. Why do people choose to blame God when bad things happen rather than blaming Satan?

Sometimes the best advice we can give in this instance is given by God in 1 Samuel 16:1, which reads as follows, "Yahweh said to Samuel, 'How long will you mourn for Saul, since I have rejected him from being king over Israel? Fill your horn with oil and go.'" In other words, let it go and move on. We will either understand it all when we get to heaven because God will explain it all to us, or God will take the memory of that painful time away from us and it will no longer matter. But brooding over a situation won't change it, so we need to trust God and move on.

Unfortunately, sometimes we don't pray because we get lazy and allow other things to crowd God out of our lives. Mark 4:19 tells us, "And the cares of this age, and the deceitfulness of riches, and the lusts of other things entering in choke the word, and it becomes unfruitful." How many times do we get up in the morning and hit the ground running? There are lunches to pack, children to get ready for school, breakfast to fix, and then off to the grind of work, where we barely have time to think, let alone pray. And after work? There is dinner to fix, homework to check, maybe some Netflix to watch and relax, and then off to bed to collapse and rest up for tomorrow, only to perform the same hectic routine all over again. Ideally, we should each start our days asking for God's blessings, guidance, and protection; and at the end of the day, we should thank him for the ways He has blessed us during the day. But how many of us actually take the time to do this? What does the Bible have to say about this?

In Mark 1:35, we read, "Early in the morning, while it was still dark, he rose up and went out, and departed into a deserted place, and prayed there." This passage is speaking about Jesus, and what's interesting is that Jesus was not even at His own home; He was staying at the house of Simon and Andrew. Jesus didn't let traveling disrupt His daily routine of prayer. Do we pray as much when we're on vacation as we do at home during our normal daily routine?

We must be intentional about having a daily prayer life. Maybe we need to keep track of how much time we waste each day. Will that movie we're watching or that video game we're playing help us make it to heaven? What about the music we listen to? To make prayer a priority, you may need to establish a definite time and place to pray. Pick somewhere free of distractions. Use a prayer journal if necessary to keep your thoughts focused. Share your desire to commit to having a daily prayer life with others to keep yourself accountable. Pray as a couple or as a family. Have a "prayer partner" if it will help.

We must remember Jesus's admonition to the scribes and Pharisees when He said, "Woe to you, scribes and Pharisees, hypocrites! For you tithe mint, dill and cumin, and have left undone the weightier matters of the law: justice, mercy and faith. But you ought to have done these and not left the other undone" (Matthew 23:23). Do we get so hung up on attending church services three times a week and "getting our time card punched," thinking that we have fulfilled God's requirements of us, that we neglect daily Bible study and prayer? All are equally important.

Or maybe we don't pray because we don't want to give up control of our lives to another being, especially one we can't see. After all, we are told from childhood, "learn to stand on your own two feet" and "look out for number one." A good example of someone not wanting to give up control of his life to God is found in the biblical story of the rich young ruler who came to Jesus to see what more he needed to do to inherit eternal life. After Jesus told him to obey the commandments and the young man said that he had, Jesus said, "If you want to be perfect, go, sell what you have, and give it to the poor, and you will have treasure in heaven; and come follow me" (Matthew 19:21). Verse 22 goes on to tell us, "But when the young man heard the saying, he went away sad, for he was one who had great possessions." Giving up his wealth would have meant giving up his comfort zone and depending upon God to supply all his needs from that day forward, something that he was not ready to do. Each of us must ponder this question: am I willing to truly give up all my wants and desires in order to seek God's will in all things? This is a test of Christian maturity.

There are several passages in the Bible that point out the fact that it is God who plans each man's life. Some of them include Job 14:5 (NIV), which says, "A person's days are determined; you have decreed the number of his months and have set limits he cannot exceed"; Proverbs 16:9, "A man's heart plans his course, but Yahweh directs his steps"; Proverbs 19:21, "There are many plans in a man's heart, but Yahweh's counsel will prevail"; and finally Proverbs 20:24, "A man's steps are from Yahweh; how then can man understand his way?" It's not wrong to plan our direction in life, but we must always be ready to submit to the will of God. It's all right to have goals for our lives, but remember, God decides if and how we will accomplish them.

Along this line, I knew since I was little that I wanted to be a nurse. My father died when I was a teenager, and my sister and I attended a (now-defunct) junior Christian college after high school. My plans were to go there, get over my shyness, and later attend a different college and get my bachelor's degree in nursing. But life—and God—has a way of changing one's plans. I didn't get to go immediately to a different college after graduation because of financial difficulties. In the end, I went to work at Willow Brook Christian Home in Delaware, Ohio, and worked as a certified nursing assistant. After three years of doing that, I became a licensed practical nurse. Seven years later, I got my associate degree in nursing and have had a varied and successful nursing career. Thirty-six years later, I still haven't gotten my bachelor's degree and no longer want it. My route to becoming a nurse was more circuitous than I had planned, but in retrospect, I wouldn't have changed a thing. Along the route that I wound up taking, I met some amazing people who have enriched my Christian life and increased my faith in God. And I can say that all along, God knew exactly what He was doing.

THOUGHT QUESTIONS

1. Do you think that you pray as often as you should? If not, why not? What do you think it would take to make prayer more of a priority in your life?

2. Do you believe that God really cares about you as an individual? Why or why not?

3. Have you ever told someone that you would pray for them and then didn't? Why not?

4. What are some things that we allow to crowd out prayer time in our lives?

5. Do your prayers lack enthusiasm? Is prayer just something to check off on a list of things to do, or is it important to you? Why did you answer the way you did?

6. Do you ever find yourself wasting time during the day? What can you do differently to live a more purposeful life?

7. Do you feel that daily Bible study and prayer are just as important as attending the services of the Lord's church three times a week? Why or why not? Do you live like you believe that they are just as important?

8. Do you know of someone who gave up on God because He didn't answer his or her prayer the way they wanted? If you could, what would you say to that person?

9. Do you believe that God has a specific purpose for your life? Why or why not?

10. Do you believe that if we could know why certain things happen, it would really make a difference in our thoughts about God? Would it lessen our pain? What would happen to our faith in this kind of circumstance? Do you think God will answer all our questions when we get to heaven, or will he erase painful memories so they no longer matter?

11. Why do you think people blame God when bad things happen instead of blaming Satan? What would you say to someone who thinks this way?

How Should We Pray and
For Whom Should We Pray?

So what is the best way to pray? Some people feel that the only worthwhile prayers are the ones where you simply say what is in your heart. Others become so concerned that they might overlook praying for something or someone; they choose to follow notes that they have made or to follow what is called a "model prayer." Any of these ways are acceptable.

Jesus gives us some advice about prayer in Matthew 6:5–8. This passage says, "When you pray, you shall not be as the hypocrites, for they love to stand and pray in the synagogues and in the corners of the streets, that they may be seen by men. Most certainly, I tell you, they have received their reward. But you, when you pray, enter into your inner room, and having shut your door, pray to your Father who is in secret, and your Father who sees in secret will reward you openly. In praying, don't use vain repetitions, as the Gentiles do; for they think that they will be heard for their much speaking. Therefore, do not be like them, for your Father knows what things you need, before you ask him." In other words, remember that you are praying to God, and for all intents and purposes, He is your primary audience even if you are giving a public prayer in a worship service, for example.

There are several model prayers: the Five-Finger Prayer, attributed to Cardinal Bergoglio before he became Pope Francis, which uses the fingers on one hand to represent those for whom you should be praying; the ACTS model prayer, which is an acronym with the letters standing for *adoration*, *confession, thanksgiving,* and *supplication*; and what we think of as the Lord's Prayer, found in Matthew 6:9–13.

The King James Version of the Lord's Prayer is the most familiar one and the one we will look at here. It says, "After this manner therefore pray ye: Our Father [which indicates a close personal relationship with God], which art In heaven [giving acknowledgment of God being above us and over us], Hallowed be thy name [giving God the glory and honor due Him], Thy kingdom come, Thy will be done in earth as it is in heaven (expressing our submission to His will in all things). Give us this day our daily bread [asking God to meet our daily needs]. And forgive our debts (asking for God's forgiveness) as we forgive our debtors [Matthew 6:14 tells us that if we don't forgive others, God will not forgive us]. And lead us not into temptation but deliver us from evil [petitioning God for His protection from the devil and the evil in this world], for Thine is the kingdom, and the power, and the glory for ever [ending our prayer with a verbalization of our awareness of the sovereignty of God]. Amen." This prayer is a gold standard and covers all areas for which we should pray.

Solomon also provided a model prayer for us in 1 Kings 8:56–61. Verse 56 focuses on God keeping His promises to His people, verse 57 asks for God's continuing presence in the lives of His people, verse 58 asks that God would give His people a continued desire to do His will, verse 59 asks that God would continue to supply the daily needs of His people, verse 60 emphasizes that there is no other god but Yahweh, and verse 61 asks for continued faithfulness of God's people in the future. I honestly had never focused much on this prayer before writing this book, but it is a beautiful prayer of supplication to God for His people.

The last type of *model prayer* is what I like to call a sentence prayer because that is exactly what it is. It is a prayer you utter while going about your daily activities and generally tends to focus on the task at hand. As an emergency room nurse, I probably say several of these in a single twelve-hour shift. A sentence prayer can be just as effective as a long drawn-out prayer. It is not unusual for me to simply pray, "Lord, this patient is critical; please help me get this IV [intravenous line] into their vein on my first attempt." I have prayed many sentence prayers standing on the ER dock waiting for emergency medical services to bring in a patient with CPR (cardiopulmonary resuscitation) in progress, asking the Lord to direct the outcome of this situation and to be with the patient's family during the difficult time. I have prayed on the helipad with patients before they were transported via air ambulance to Nashville with families as they have struggled to accept a loved one's prognosis and with patients who have faced their own crises, sometimes even unrelated to their health. I have concluded during my nursing career that I cannot make it through a single minute of a single day without God by my side! Life is just too hard sometimes, and unfortunately, as a nurse, I usually see people on the worst days of their lives.

What other specifics are there as to how to pray? First, we must pray in Jesus's name. John 14:13–14 tells us, "Whatever you will ask *in my name*, I will do it, that the Father may be glorified in the Son. If you ask anything *in my name*, I will do it" (emphasis mine). We do not pray to Jesus or Mary, the mother of Jesus, but we pray to God the Father through and in Jesus's name. Praying in Jesus's name implies praying in the will of Jesus and God. We are praying that God's will might be done in this particular situation.

Ephesians 6:18 also tells us, "And pray in the Spirit on all occasions with all kinds of prayers and requests. With this in mind, be alert and always keep on praying for the Lord's people." We must always pray in the Spirit, remembering that God is a spirit. Jude 1:20 also says, "But you, beloved, keep building up yourselves on your most holy faith, praying in the Holy Spirit." Praying in the Spirit means that the Spirit will carry our prayers to the throne of God. (We will look at this in more depth later.)

Later chapters in this study guide will focus on what keeps God from hearing our prayers and why God might reject our prayers. For now, let's focus on for whom we should pray.

Luke 6:28 says, "Bless those who curse you, and pray for those who mistreat you." A perfect example of this (other than Jesus's prayer for the people crucifying Him when He was on the cross) is found in Numbers 12:1–15. Moses prayed for his sister Miriam, who was stricken with leprosy by God for being jealous of her brother Moses because he was recognized as a prophet of God, but she and Aaron were not for speaking out against Moses's Cushite wife. Despite her behavior, Moses prayed to God for Miriam and asked God to heal her of her leprosy. Do we pray for those who wrong us or talk badly about us? Moses himself gave us a good example of how we should react to others who mistreat us. Do you find it easy or hard to follow his example?

Matthew 5:43–48 says, "You have heard that it was said, 'You shall love your neighbor and hate your enemy.' But I tell you, love your enemies, bless those who curse you, do good to those who hate you, and pray for those who mistreat you and persecute you, that you may be children of your Father who is in heaven. For he makes his sun to rise on the evil and the good, and sends rain on the just and the unjust. For if you love those who love you, what reward do you have? Don't even the tax collectors do the same? If you only greet your friends, what more do you do than others? Don't even the tax collectors do the same? Therefore you shall be perfect, as your Father in heaven is perfect."

If we can pray for people who mistreat us and speak badly of us and not seek revenge, which would be the natural human thing to do, we are on our way to becoming more Christlike and true children of God. But boy, is it hard! Sometimes we must pray for the strength to pray for our enemies! I know that I have felt better when I do try to pray for people who have been mean to me (you can see a lot of that in the emergency department at the hospital when people are hurting and sick and impatient and don't want to wait their turn), but sometimes it is still difficult. Sometimes I must remind myself that they are all God's children, and I make a conscious decision to pray for them during those times. It's true: you can get very jaded working in an emergency department, and I must constantly guard against this. It's called "compassion fatigue." When I find myself slipping, I pray even harder.

We should also pray for our friends in the church. We read in the book of James 5:16, "Confess your offenses to one another, and pray for one another, that you may be healed." We all need the prayers of others, and they need our prayers too.

Please note what the Bible says in Job 42:10 (NIV), "After Job had prayed for his friends, the Lord restored his fortunes and gave him twice as much." Even though Job was wealthier after his suffering, we are not to pray for others because of what we might get out of it. We pray for others out of love for them and concern for what they are going through. We then leave the outcome up to God.

We need to pray for our families. Again, Job is a prime example. Job 1:4–5 says, "His sons went and held a feast in the house of each one on his birthday; and they sent and called for their three sisters to eat and drink with them. It was so, when the days of their feasting had run their course, that Job sent and sanctified them, and rose up early in the morning, and offered burnt offerings according to the number of them all. For Job said, 'It may be that my sons have sinned, and renounced God in their hearts.' Job did so continually." As we pointed out in one of the previous chapters, do we pray for our children and grandchildren? We should. Sometimes it's easy to take those closest to us for granted, but we need to pray for them. And those closest to you may be the most difficult for you to talk to about their eternal destiny because you might fear straining that relationship, but it is your closeness to them that makes you the perfect person to discuss this with them. If you don't talk to them about eternity, who will? Pray for your children, your grandchildren, and your spouse.

We should pray for ourselves. Psalm 51:1–4 is a perfect example of a scripture we can pray to God. It says, "Have mercy on me, God, according to your loving kindness. According to the multitude of your tender mercies, blot out my transgressions. My sin is constantly before me. Against you, and you only, I have sinned, and done that which is evil in your sight; that you may be proved right when you speak, and justified when you judge." We need to pray for strength, the forgiveness of our sins, compassion, guidance, and internal peace to name a few things.

The Bible teaches that we should pray for our fellowmen and those over us. In 1 Timothy 2:1–2, we read, "I exhort therefore, first of all, that petitions, prayers, intercessions and giving of thanks be made for all men; for kings and all who are in high places, that we may lead a quiet and tranquil life in all godliness and reverence." Do we pray for those over us in our church congregations, the elders and deacons? Do we think to pray for those over us in government and for the leaders of other countries? Do we pray that no laws will be enacted that forbid us to assemble and worship God in the future? Anything is possible in this crazy messed-up world, and we need to pray for God's continued blessing on His church and for His people.

We need to pray for evangelistic efforts as in 2 Thessalonians 3:1, which says, "Finally, brothers, pray for us, that the word of the Lord may be spread rapidly and be glorified, even as also with you," and for the lost as in Acts 26:18, "To open their eyes, that they may turn from darkness to light and from the power of Satan to God, that they may receive remission of sins and an inheritance among those who are sanctified by faith in me." One of the Christians' most important purposes here on earth is to lead the lost to Christ, but I fear that some of us tend to take that responsibility too lightly. We need to live like we are going to die tomorrow and get serious about evangelism, especially to those with whom we have daily contact! Remember we are only commissioned to spread the Gospel; the outcome is up to the individual.

The apostle Paul frequently mentions prayer in his letters, and many times he prayed for people he didn't even know. But they were his brothers and sisters in Christ, and to Paul, that is what made the difference. We too should pray for our brothers and sisters in foreign lands, especially those undergoing hardships and persecution for their beliefs. Please note that people tend to be more receptive to the Gospel when they are undergoing a crisis in their lives. After all, many people think that they "don't need God" when things are going well for them. If we pray that God will open someone's heart to Jesus, do we realize that sometimes our friends might have to undergo a personal crisis in their life for that to happen? We need to be aware of that possibility and be willing to stand by and help our friend should it become necessary to do so.

The apostle James tells us in James 5:14–15 that we should pray for the sick: "Is any among you sick? Let him call for the elders of the assembly, and let them pray over him, anointing him with oil in the name of the Lord, and the prayer of faith will heal him who is sick and the Lord will raise him up." When we pray for healing for a Christian brother or sister, we need to realize that healing might come in this life or in the next. Just because a brother or sister dies doesn't mean that God didn't heal them. Actually, He did!

We must also pray purposely. Have you ever thought about the difficult position we can put God in simply with our prayers? What if a couple is praying for beautiful sunshine for their weekend wedding and a local farmer is praying for rain lest he lose his crops? What about when two football teams are playing against each other for a football championship and their fans are praying for victory for their team? Speaking of which, what about prayers offered before a football game so that no one gets hurt, and then you have two teams on the field whose members are trying to hit each other's team members as hard as possible? Have we ever considered how ridiculous some of our prayers must seem to God?

What about the people who pray before a NASCAR race that God will keep the drivers, who are going to be driving their race cars over a hundred miles per hour, safe? Do they just expect God to suspend the laws of nature for a few minutes? I mean, here are grown men taking huge risks and asking for deliverance from the consequences of their actions. Is that right in God's eyes?

No matter whether you choose to follow a model prayer or simply pray from the heart, the most important thing obviously is to pray to God daily. God is always present, always ready and willing to listen. He never sleeps, and He will never forsake those who diligently seek Him in prayer. Commit to setting some time aside every day and pray to God to let Him know what is on your heart.

THOUGHT QUESTIONS

1. Do you think that we are meant to just pray what is on our hearts or is OK to follow a model prayer? Why do you think the way you do? Which method do you use? Have you ever changed up the way you pray—praying from the heart one time and following a model prayer the next time? Why or why not? Would following a model prayer help you remember to pray for things that you might sometimes overlook?

2. Do you find it easier or harder to pray for yourself or others? Why?

3. The next time you hear someone pray, pay close attention. Do they seem to be praying from the heart or following a model prayer?

4. For whom should we be praying? How many times do we think to pray for fellow Christians in other countries?

5. Is there someone that you know personally for whom you should be praying that they come to know the Lord Jesus before it is everlastingly too late? Is this person on your daily prayer list? Why or why not? Even if you feel that this person might not be ready to listen to you now if you try to talk with them about their eternal destiny, you could still pray that God would open his or her heart to Him. Do you believe this? Can you pray for this?

6. Do you believe that God answers our prayers for healing for a Christian brother or sister if He decides to take them home to heaven instead of healing them here on earth?

LESSON 5

What Keeps God From Hearing Our Prayers?

THERE ARE THINGS, UNFORTUNATELY, THAT WE DO, WHICH MIGHT KEEP God from answering our prayers the way we would like Him to; but we will address these in a future chapter. For right now, let us focus on what might keep God from hearing our prayers in the first place. And it basically boils down to one thing: disobedience.

The writer of Proverb 28:9 says, "He who turns his ear away from hearing the law, even his prayer is an abomination." If we are not trying to live our lives the way God wants us to, He will not hear our prayers.

The apostle John tells us in his Gospel, John 15:7, "If you remain in me, and my words remain in you, you will ask whatever you desire, and it will be done for you." God will not hear our prayers if we are not trying to keep His commandments. Don't do the things He finds pleasing, don't believe in Jesus, and don't love one another. The only way for God to hear our prayers is to live in obedience to Him.

John reiterates this thought in 1 John 3:21– 23, "Beloved, if our hearts don't condemn us, we have boldness toward God; so whatever we ask, we receive from him, because we keep his commandments and do the things that are pleasing in his sight. This is his commandment, that we should believe in the name of his Son, Jesus Christ, and love one another, even as he commanded."

The Bible points out quite obviously that God will not hear the prayers of the wicked. Psalm 66:18, says, "If I had cherished sin in my heart, the

Lord wouldn't have listened." Proverbs 15:29 adds, "Yahweh is far from the wicked, but he hears the prayers of the righteous." Proverbs 1:28–30 shows that God will wash His hands of those who choose not to follow His ways; this passage says, "Then they will call on me, but I will not answer. They will seek me diligently, but they will not find me; because they hated knowledge and didn't choose the fear of Yahweh. They wanted none of my counsel. They despised all my reproof. Therefore, they will eat of the fruit of their own way, and be filled with their own schemes." Continuing this theme, we read in Isaiah 59:2, "But your iniquities have separated you and your God, and your sins have hidden his face from you, so that he will not hear." In the New Testament, Peter wrote in 1 Peter 3:12, "For the eyes of the Lord are on the righteous, and his ears open to their prayer; but the face of the Lord is against those who do evil."

The Bible is full of examples of sinful men who prayed to God and whose prayers were not acknowledged because of the sinfulness of the one praying or the people involved. Simply put, we cannot continue in sin and expect God to hear our prayers. The Bible is very plain about this.

Joshua 7:1–26 tells of a time when some of the Israelites disobeyed God and as a result, God refused to listen to the prayers of Joshua. Verse 1 says, "But the children of Israel committed a trespass in the devoted things; for Achan, the son of Carmi, the son of Zabdi, the son of Zerah, of the tribe of Judah, took some of the devoted things. Therefore, Yahweh's anger burned against the children of Israel."

After this, the men of Israel went to fight against the men of Ai and were defeated. Starting in verse 6 of this same chapter we read, "Then Joshua tore his clothes and fell down before the ark of the Lord, saying, 'Alas, Lord Yahweh, why have you brought this people over the Jordan at all, to deliver us into the hands of the Amorites, to cause us to perish? I wish that we had been content and lived beyond the Jordan! Oh, Lord, what shall I say, after Israel has turned their backs before their enemies! For the Canaanites and all the inhabitants of the land will hear of it, and surround us, and cut off our name from the earth. What will you do for your great name?' Yahweh said to Joshua, 'Get up! Why have you fallen on your face like that? Israel has sinned. Yes, they have even transgressed my covenant which I commanded them. Yes, they have even taken some of the devoted things, and have also stolen, and have also deceived. They have even put it among their own stuff. Therefore the children of Israel can't stand before their enemies. They turn their backs before their enemies, because they have become devoted for destruction. I will not be with you any more, unless you destroy the devoted things from among you.'" (Joshua 7:6–12)

Sin had to be removed from the people's lives, and they had to come back to God with sincere, repentant hearts before He would listen to their prayers. In verses 24–26, we learn that "Joshua, and all of Israel with him, took Achan the son of Zerah, the silver, the robe, the wedge of gold, his sons, his daughters, his cattle, his donkeys, his sheep, his tent and all that he had; and they brought them up to the valley of Achor. Joshua said, 'Why have you troubled us? Yahweh will trouble you today.' All Israel stoned him with stones, and they burned them with fire and stoned them with stones. They raised over him a great heap of stones that remains to this day. Yahweh turned from the fierceness of his anger. Therefore the name of that place was called 'The valley of Achor" to this day.'" When I read this story, I was struck by how seriously the Lord takes disobedience. Even Achan's family, his livestock, and his tent were burned! God didn't want any trace of Achan's existence left! Even his family and livestock had to pay the penalty for his sin.

Another example from the Old Testament is King Saul. After Samuel, the prophet, had died, the Philistine army set up camp at Shunem to fight against the nation of Israel. Saul was afraid; 1 Samuel 28:5 says, "When Saul inquired of Yahweh, Yahweh didn't answer him by dreams, by Urim, or by prophets." Then Saul turned to a medium, which is defined as "one who consults the dead on behalf of the living." Why did God not answer the prayers of Saul? It all goes back to an earlier passage in 1 Samuel 13:5–14, which tells of the time Saul grew impatient waiting for Samuel to come and bless his troops before going into battle. Therefore, Saul took it upon himself to offer the burnt offering, which he did not have the right to do. Verses 13–14 in this passage say, "Samuel said to Saul, 'You have done foolishly. You have not kept the commandment of Yahweh your God, which he commanded you; for now Yahweh would have established your kingdom on Israel forever. But your kingdom will not continue." Because of his sinfulness, Saul lost his kingdom.

There is an interesting passage in the New Testament that I would like us to examine now. It's found in the Gospel of John and tells of a time when the Pharisees were questioning a man who had been blind since birth. Jesus healed the man on the Sabbath, and the Pharisees wanted to know how he had been healed. The man who had been healed said in John 9:30–31, "How amazing! You don't know where he comes from, yet he opened my eyes. We know that God doesn't listen to sinners, but if anyone is a worshipper of God, and does his will, he listens to him."

OK, so this passage says that God doesn't hear the prayer of sinners, right? A sinner is someone who does not do the will of God, agreed? So how do we explain Acts 10:1–47? This is the story of Cornelius, described in verses 1–2 as the following: "Now there was a certain man in Caesarea, Cornelius by name, a centurion of what was called the Italian Regiment, a devout man, and one who feared God with all his house, who gave gifts for the needy generously to the people, and always prayed to God." One day, an angel appeared to Cornelius and told him that God had taken note of his prayers and gifts to the needy and that he was to send to Joppa and ask a man named Peter to visit him. At the same time, Peter saw a vision telling him to eat all manner of animals, birds, and reptiles and God told him that some men had come seeking him and that he was to go with them to Joppa. Once there, Peter preached the Word of God to Cornelius and his household, and they were all baptized. Now my question is, if God doesn't hear the prayers of sinners (and Cornelius was a Gentile and not a brother in Christ), why did God hear his prayers? What made the difference in the prayers of Cornelius versus other nonbelievers who prayed to God? I believe the answer is that God knew that Cornelius was praying from a humble and sincere heart, diligently seeking the Lord of heaven and earth. Do you agree or disagree?

My father-in-law was a very sweet man, a stereotypical Italian, loud, proud of his family, and emotional. He took a lot of getting used to from someone who was once as shy as I was! But from day one, he treated me like a daughter, not just a daughter-in-law. I was very lucky when it came to my in-laws. I loved them both dearly.

But one thing bothered me about Pete, even up until the day he died. He was not religious, in the strictest sense of the word. In the twenty-three years I knew him, he never attended a worship service nor read his Bible. And yet, every night he would get on his knees beside his bed and pray to God. It wasn't any good trying to talk to Pete about church. He didn't believe in "organized religion." He never saw the point of going to church. But he believed that God heard his prayers. I often wondered why he felt that he could pray to God, but he didn't see the need to worship Him. In later years, I learned to my surprise that many people feel this way.

People love to quote a passage from 2 Chronicles 7:14, using it to ask God to heal the United States of America. Unfortunately, all too often, they choose to overlook the conditions God sets out for this healing. The passage in question says, "If my people, who are called by my name, will humble themselves, pray, seek my face, and turn from their wicked ways, then I will hear from heaven, will forgive their sin, and heal their land." The conditions God has laid down are very explicit: this land and its people must humble themselves before God (acknowledging Him as their master and Lord), must pray, seek His face, (repent), and turn from their wicked ways. *Then* God says that he will heal their land. People aren't willing to accept God's conditions; they want to continue living in sin, do their own thing, and expect God to bless this land. In that case, God will not bless this country or any nation that refuses to acknowledge God as the Creator of the universe, the one to whom all reverence is due and the Savior of the world. It all boils down to this one Bible verse: "Blessed is the nation whose God is Yahweh, the people whom he has chosen for his own inheritance" (Psalm 33:12). With homosexuality, transgenderism, and abortion (to name a few things) being widely accepted in this country, why would God bless us? For God to hear our prayers, we must address any unforgiven sin in our lives and remove it, repenting and confessing to God our sinfulness and be willing to accept His help in doing better in the future.

THOUGHT QUESTIONS

1. Do you believe that God hears the prayers of every unbeliever? Why or why not?

2. Have you ever experienced a time when you prayed for something or someone and just did not feel that God heard you? Why do you think that you felt that way? Do you think that there might have been something in your life that might have prevented God from hearing your prayer? Did you do anything about it?

3. In 2 Chronicles, we read about a wicked king named Manasseh. Second Chronicles 33:2 says, "He did that which was evil in Yahweh's sight, after the abominations of the nations whom Yahweh cast out before the children of Israel." Read verses 9–20 and see if you can figure out why God might have listened to the prayers of such an evil man. What did you discover?

4. Do you believe that God will bless the United States of America with the way things stand now? What must change before we can expect this country to receive God's blessings? What can we, as individuals, do about this?

5. What keeps God from hearing the prayers of individuals?

41

LESSON 6

How Does God Answer Our Prayers?

OK, WE HAVE ALREADY STUDIED THE FIVE DIFFERENT TYPES OF PRAYERS, reasons why we should pray, reasons why we don't pray, how we should pray and for whom, and what keeps God from hearing our prayers. But now the burning question is, just how does God answer our prayers? How do we know what His answer is? After all, the Bible tells us in Proverbs 16:9, "A man's heart plans his course, but Yahweh directs his steps." How do we *know* how God wants us to proceed?

Obviously in the Bible, we read several stories of people who spoke directly to God and to whom God spoke directly in return. Adam and Eve, Moses, Ezekiel, Noah, Job, Isaiah, and on and on. But you would be hard-pressed to find anyone in this day and age who has actually heard the voice of God, so how do we get the answers to our prayers? How does God *speak* to us today?

One way that God can speak to us is by simply planting a thought in our minds. This happened to me while I was writing this book. I planned this book before the COVID pandemic struck, and I had it organized to the smallest detail on file cards. As I was finalizing it, though, a thought came to me one night as I was trying to go to sleep. The thought was this, *You have written lessons on different kinds of prayers and when God says yes or no, but you have not specifically addressed how God answers our prayers.* Thus at the last minute as I was polishing my final draft, this chapter came to be.

Another way we can receive an answer to a prayer is simply through circumstances. Perhaps we have prayed for someone to be healed of an illness, and they were. That is obviously an answer to a prayer.

On the flip side, if we pray for a Christian who is struggling with an illness and they are not cured but dies instead, are they not "healed" now in the strictest sense of the word since they are once again whole and well and dwelling with Jesus in paradise? I have several Christian friends who are limited in their mobility and confined to wheelchairs, but the greatest blessing will be when they are released from those bonds and free to walk about again in eternity. That would, indeed, be the perfect answer to many prayers offered on their behalf because they *would be* "healed" and whole again.

My older brother, Steve, was physically and mentally disabled since birth. He struggled to learn, to walk, to control his emotions. Mentally, he had the mind of a five-year-old, especially in his later years. For the last few years of his life, he was confined to a wheelchair, my dear brother who used to walk two or three miles to the library in our hometown to check out books to read. Reading was his passion. Late in life, many times, he talked about the things he "could no longer do." When he lay dying in the nursing home, his heart and single kidney shutting down for all eternity, my sister sat with him and told him about all the things that he was going to be able to do once again in heaven.

"You'll be able to hear, and talk plainly, and run and walk again, and you will never hurt or be sad again." At our request, Steve finally let go and joined our parents in eternity on Jan's and my birthday, giving us the greatest, most bittersweet present he could give. His birthday present to us was knowing that he was finally free of his bondage and completely whole again.

Sometimes the Lord uses circumstances to point us in the direction in which He wants us to go.

My husband laughs at me, but when I have a decision to make, I pray, "Lord, if the outcome matters to what You want me to do, please make that choice so obvious to me that I cannot miss Your will for my life." And you know, He does! Perhaps I'm trying to decide whether to stay in one job or take another, and the circumstances overwhelmingly point to one choice over the other. I truly believe that you *can* know God's will for your life if you pray and open your heart to His answer. The Lord has never failed me yet! But you must be willing to be watchful for His answer so you don't miss what He is trying to tell you.

What are some other ways that God can "tell" us His answers to our prayers? For one, He can speak to us in dreams. The Bible is filled with stories of people to whom God spoke in dreams—Joseph in the Old Testament (Genesis 37:5–7); Abimelech (Genesis 20:3); Solomon (1 Kings 3:5–28); Joseph, Jesus's stepfather in the New Testament (Matthew 1:20–21 and 2:13); the three Magi (Matthew 2:12); the apostle Paul (Acts 16:9, 10); and even Pilate's wife (Matthew 27:19).

God also tells us His will by the leadings of the Holy Spirit. The apostle John says in his Gospel, John 16:13–15, "However when he, the Spirit of truth, has come, he will guide you into all truth, for he will not speak from himself, but whatever he hears, he will speak. He will declare to you things that are coming." God sent the Holy Spirit to be our guide in our day-to-day lives.

Jesus goes on to assure His apostles in Luke 12:11–12, "When they bring you before the synagogues, the rulers, and the authorities, don't be anxious how or what you will answer, or what you will say, for the Holy Spirit will teach you in that same hour what you must say." The apostles had the assurance that the Holy Spirit would direct their speech. They didn't have to worry about what to say or how to say it. All they had to do was open their mouths and let the Holy Spirit speak for them.

Paul, Timothy, and Silas were once forbidden by the Holy Spirit to go where they wanted. We read about this incident in Acts 16:6, which says, "When they had gone through the region of Phrygia and Galatia, they were forbidden by the Holy Spirit to speak the word in Asia." Why were they forbidden to go to Asia? Some commentaries say that God wanted Peter to preach to the Gentiles in Asia while Paul and his companions were to concentrate on preaching to the Jews. To follow the leadings of the Holy Spirit, we must pray and be open to His prompts, just as the apostles were. If we pray and feel overwhelmingly pulled or pushed in a certain direction, we need to heed that prompt. I don't really believe in coincidence, do you?

Another way in which God might reveal His will for our lives is through the counsel of others. Perhaps we are struggling with a decision and don't know which way to turn. The Bible teaches us that "the way of a fool is right in his own eyes, but he who is wise listens to counsel" (Proverbs 12:15). Wise people seek the advice of other Christians, especially when they are struggling with an issue. Who better to go to for advice than one of your brothers or sisters in Christ? We are God's family, and we need to look out for one another as a family.

Another way that God might speak to us is through the words of others. Have you ever heard a sermon that just seemed to address something with which you had been struggling? Coincidence? I think not. Have you ever heard a sermon and thought that the preacher was speaking directly to you, that what he was saying was something that you needed to hear at that particular time of your life? After all, God used the words of Peter to convict the people of their sins on the day of Pentecost in Acts 2:37–41, which says, "Now when they heard this, they were cut to the heart, and said to Peter and the rest of the apostles, 'Brothers, what shall we do?' Peter said to them, 'Repent, and be baptized, every one of you, in the name of Jesus Christ for the forgiveness of sins, and you will receive the gift of the Holy Spirit. For the promise is to you, and your children, and to all who are far off, even as many as the Lord our God will call to himself.' With many other words he testified, and exhorted them, saying, 'Save yourself from this crooked generation!' Then those who gladly received his word were baptized. There were added that day about three thousand souls." God used the words of Peter's sermon to convict the people of their sins. Not only that, but God also uses the consciences of people to convict them of their wrongdoings.

God even speaks through creation, especially if you are seeking peace and solitude. Perhaps you are feeling overwhelmed by the day-to-day struggle of life and simply want some comfort from the heavenly Father. Psalm 19:1–4 eloquently says, "The heavens declare the glory of God. The expanse shows his handiwork. Day after day they poured out speech, and night after night they display knowledge. There is no speech or language, where their voice is not heard. Their voice has gone out through all the earth, their words to the end of the world." A good exercise to do is to find a quiet spot to contemplate something small and insignificant: a blade of grass, a leaf, a honeybee. Free your mind of all that is pressing in on you. Study this piece of nature. Pause and allow God to fill your mind with what He wants.

Another verse that points out beautifully how God speaks through his creation is found in Romans 1:20 (NIV), which says, "For since the creation of the world God's invisible qualities—his eternal power and divine nature—have clearly been seen, being understood from what was made, so that people are without excuse." How people can look at the beauty that surrounds them in this world and not realize the presence of a Creator is beyond me. There is no way this earth came about by a haphazard bang and everything just fell into place. To me, it takes more gall to believe that than it takes faith to believe in a Creator.

God can even answer our prayers through our thoughts. Romans 12:2 tells us, "Don't be conformed to this world, but be transformed by the renewing of your mind, so that you may prove what is the good, well-pleasing and perfect will of God is." How do we discover what the will of God is? By praying, being aware of the leading of the Holy Spirit, looking at our circumstances, paying attention to our dreams, seeking the godly counsel of others, listening to sermons, and by getting back to nature.

And lastly, God speaks to us through His Word, the Bible. While seeking God's will, we need to pray and meditate upon His Word. Have you ever read a particular passage, perhaps one that you have read many times before and are quite familiar with, and all of a sudden, some seemingly insignificant detail just leaped from the page to your consciousness? Something that you have never even considered before despite the number of times you might have read that passage? That's called an "aha moment."

That's why, when I am studying my Bible, I like to read from different versions. Sometimes something will catch my attention and I will think, *I don't remember reading that before*, so I will check a more familiar version, and lo and behold, there it is! Reading a different version of the Bible might present you with a different viewpoint than you had previously considered, or it might cause you to think more deeply about a passage that you thought you already knew backward and forward. Or it might bring out a detail that you had never considered before. In that moment, God might be trying to speak to you through His Word. Stop. Meditate on that scripture. See if you can deduce what it is God might be trying to tell you.

One of the most powerful scripture passages about the Word of God is found in 2 Timothy 3:16–17, which says, "Every scripture is God-breathed and profitable for teaching, for reproof, for correction, and for instruction in righteousness, that each person who belongs to God may be complete, thoroughly equipped for every good work." God gave His people His Word, the Bible, to enable us to live as He would have us do on a day-to-day basis. If every other book in the world were destroyed, the Bible would still be all we would need.

Psalm 119:105 points out to us (and God) that "your word is a lamp to my feet, and a light for my path." God's Word tells us where to go and how to get there. It provides us with guidance and direction.

Continuing on this theme, one of the most beautiful passages that address this issue is found in the Gospel of John 14:1–6, which says, "'Don't let your hearts be troubled. Believe in God. Believe also in me. In my Father's house are many homes. If it weren't so, I would have told you. I am going to prepare a place for you. If I go and prepare a place for you, I will come again, and receive you to myself, that where I am, you may be there also. You know where I go, and you know the way.' Thomas said to him, 'Lord, we don't know where you are going. How can we know the way?' Jesus said to him, 'I am the way, the truth and the life. No one comes to the Father, except through me.'" The only way to heaven is through Jesus and by His Word.

God uses His Word to work in the lives of believers. We are told this in 1 Thessalonians 2:13, which reads as follows, "For this cause we also thank God without ceasing, that when you received from us the word of the message of God, you accepted it not as the word of men, but as it is in truth, the word of God, which also works in you who believe." God's Word is truth.

Hebrews 4:12 says, "For the word of God is living and active, and sharper than any two-edged sword, piercing even to the dividing of soul and spirit, of both joints and marrow, and is able to discern the thoughts and intentions of the heart." God's Word is powerful and is one way He speaks to us and shows us what His will for our lives is.

THOUGHT QUESTIONS

1. Do you believe that God can speak to His people today? Why or why not?

2. In how many ways can God speak to His people? How many have you experienced?

3. What must you do to be receptive to hearing God speak to you?

4. Do you believe that it is OK to read different versions of the Bible? Why or why not? What would be the advantage of doing so? What would be a disadvantage?

LESSON 7

When God's Answer Is No

IN THE LAST CHAPTER, WE LEARNED THAT DISOBEDIENCE CAN PREVENT God from hearing our prayers. In this chapter, we are going to learn some reasons why God might answer no to our prayers.

While I was writing this chapter, Rodney, one of our ministers, was speaking one night. He made the following comment: "There is no such thing as unanswered prayers." I wrote that comment on a note card and took it home to study it. And study it I did. I studied that thought for a total of forty-three days. It shook my thinking to my core. For years, I had thought that prayers that I had prayed—"God, please let this relationship work out. I am so in love,""God, please heal my friend"—which didn't work out were because they were unanswered prayers. After Rodney's sermon, though, I came to understand that they were not unanswered prayers, but prayers in which God had simply said no to my requests.

I remember some thirty-some years ago, hearing several young people discussing Psalm 37:4, which says, "Also delight yourself in Yahweh, and he will give you the desires of your heart." These young adults were taking this passage to mean that one could ask God for anything, and He was *obligated* to give it to you. First, God is not obligated to do anything for us; and secondly, there are several reasons why God might say no to our prayers. This chapter deals with those reasons.

The Bible tells us that we must pray, *believing* that God will hear us and that He *will* answer our prayers. James tells us in James 1:6–8, "But let him ask in faith, without any doubting, for he who doubts is like a wave of the sea, driven by the wind and tossed. For that man shouldn't think that he will receive anything from the Lord. He is a double-minded man, unstable in all his ways." Notice that faith must come from the one praying. Some televangelists who say that a person they are praying over for healing "doesn't have enough faith" need to reexamine this passage. It is not the one who is seeking healing must have faith but the one doing the praying!

Matthew 21:22 says, "All things, whatever you ask in prayer, believing, you will receive." Again, that seems like a clear promise from God, doesn't it? All we must do is ask and believe, right? On the other hand, though, God has laid down some other ground rules for receiving that for which we are praying.

First, you must pray with pure motives. Again, James has something to say about this in his epistle, James 4:2–3, which read, "You lust and don't have. You murder and covet, and can't obtain. You fight and make war. You don't have because you don't ask. You ask and don't receive, because you ask with wrong motives, so that you may spend it on your pleasures." What would be *wrong motives*? This verse tells us, "So that you may spend it on your pleasures." Consider people who play the lottery and pray that they have the winning tickets. Why do they generally want to win? Was it to buy a bigger house, a new car, to live a life of leisure, and never have to work again? Wouldn't that be *spending it on your pleasures*? How many people have won a huge jackpot and then you learn later that all that money ruined their lives? Why? It's because they weren't disciplined, money didn't bring them happiness, and many times they were worshipping their riches instead of almighty God. We need to ask ourselves, "Why am I praying for this?" After all, it is entirely possible to pray for something that is not good for you, and God knows what is best. Face it, if you want God to do what is best for you, winning the lottery is probably not in your future.

Proverb 16:2 says, "All the ways of a man are clean in his own eyes; but Yahweh weighs the motives." Along that same line, Proverbs 21:2 says essentially the same thing: "Every way of a man is right in his own eyes, but Yahweh weighs the hearts." God knows why we pray for certain things, and if our motives are not good ones, He will probably say no to our prayers.

The Gospel of John gives us another reason God might say no to our prayers, and it's found in John 14:13–14. These verses say, "Whatever you will ask in my name, I will do it, that the Father may be glorified in the Son. If you will ask anything in my name, I will do." There are two reasons given in this passage why God might say no to our prayers: (1) that for which we pray must bring glory to God and (2) we must ask in Jesus's name, which also implies in the will of Jesus. Can you see how praying for something might not be in the will of Jesus?

Everything we do is to be to the glory of God. First Corinthians 10:31 says, "Whether therefore you eat, or drink, or whatever you do, do all to the glory of God." We need to ask ourselves, "Is what I'm praying for going to bring glory to God?" If not, our motives are wrong, and we are probably not going to receive that for which we are praying.

Those things for which we are praying also need to be compliant with the will of God. Remember we don't see things from the same perspective that God does. Our viewpoints tend to be more personal, selfish, and finite. We can't see into the future, and we can't see the big picture the same way God can. In later chapters, we will discuss what happens when we don't submit to the will of God and how to submit to the will of God.

On a side note, there are at least two examples given in the Bible when someone changed God's intentions. The first one was in the book of Exodus 32:11–14, which we already examined in chapter 1 of this study guide. In this passage, God was ready to destroy the Israelite nation for their constant moaning and groaning, and Moses talked God out of it. Moses pointed out to God in this passage that God had made a covenant with Abraham, Isaac, and Israel to make a great nation out of the Israelite people; and if He wiped them off the face of the earth, the Egyptians would say that God had simply brought His people out to the desert to bring evil upon them. We know from reading this passage that God relented and did not destroy the Israelite nation.

The second example is found in the book of 2 Kings 20:1–6, which reads, "In those days Hezekiah was sick and dying. Isaiah the prophet, the son of Amoz, came to him, and said to him, 'Yahweh says, "Set your house in order; for you will die, and not live."' Then he turned his face to the wall, and prayed to Yahweh, saying, 'Remember now, Yahweh, I beg you, how I have walked before you in truth and with a perfect heart, and done that which is good in your sight.' And Hezekiah wept bitterly. Before Isaiah had gone out in the middle part of the city, Yahweh's word came to him, saying, 'Turn back and tell Hezekiah the prince of my people, "Yahweh, the God of David your father, says, 'I have heard your prayer. I have seen your tears. Behold, I will heal you. On the third day you will go up to Yahweh's house. I will add to your days fifteen years.'" Because Hezekiah prayed and wept before God, God decided to heal him of his illness and allow him to live another fifteen years.

While these two examples show us that we can pray and God *may* change His mind, He still has the final say. Again, we read in 1 John 5:14– 15, "This is the boldness which we have toward him, that if we ask anything according to his will, he listens to us. And if we know that he listens to us, whatever we ask, we know that we have the petitions which we have asked of him." We can ask for what we want, but we must submit to the will of God as we pray.

Stop and think about something for a moment: what if the things we are praying for are not in our best interests at all? Again, this goes back to the fact that God can see the big picture and we can't. Have you ever prayed for something you thought you wanted, but it didn't come to fruition? After some time had passed, you realized that it was best that you did not receive the thing you had thought you wanted. Perhaps this is what Jesus is referring to in Matthew 7:9–11 when He said, "Or who is there among you, who, if his son asks him for bread, will give him a stone? Or if he asks for a fish, who will give him a serpent? If you then, being evil, know how to give good gifts to your children, how much more will your Father who is in heaven give good things to those who ask him!" These may refer to times when we think that we are praying for things we need (fish and bread), but God knows that the things we are really asking for are analogous to snakes and stones. Maybe God, who understands our situations and our hearts, knows that what we *think* we want isn't what we really want or need.

And probably the best reason of all why God might say no to our prayers—because He is the Creator of the universe and the one who blesses each of us more than we deserve, doesn't God have the *right* to say no? After all, God said in Job 38:4–7, "Where were you when I laid the foundations of the earth? Declare, if you have understanding. Who determined its measures, if you know? Or who stretched the line on it? Whereupon was its foundations fastened? Or who laid its cornerstone, when the morning stars sang together, and all the sons of God shouted for joy?" Who are we to question the God of the universe? What gives us the audacity to feel like we have the right to do so?

God does not always answer yes to our prayers. When we pray for something, we should believe that He hears us and that He has the power to say *yes if* He wants. But we must also pray with pure motives and pray for things that will bring honor to God. We also must pray for God's will to be done in our lives—in the big things and the little ones. When we pray with the right attitude, we are putting ourselves under God's control, in His will, and expressing His sovereignty over us.

THOUGHT QUESTIONS

1. Do you believe that there is such a thing as *unanswered prayers*? Why or why not?

2. Has there ever been a time in your past when you really wanted something and God said no, and now looking back, you realize that God was right and that He gave you something even better in the end? Has that experience helped you learn to trust God even more in the future? Have you ever thanked God for answering no to a prayer?

3. What are some things that can keep God from answering our prayers the way we want?

4. Do you believe that God has the right to say no to any of our prayers? Why or why not?

5. Can you think of other people in the Bible who prayed for something and God's answer was no?

LESSON 8

To Whom Did God Say No in the Bible?

WHO WERE SOME OF THE PEOPLE IN THE BIBLE WHO PRAYED FOR something and God said no to their requests? What can we learn about the reasons why God might have answered their prayers the way He did? And what can we learn about these people's responses to God's answer of no?

As we learned in a previous chapter, disobedience can keep God from answering our prayers (see 1 John 3:22–23). The following story from the Old Testament perfectly illustrates this.

The first person who comes to mind is King David in the Old Testament. In 2 Samuel 12:13–23, the Bible says, "David said to Nathan, 'I have sinned against Yahweh.' Nathan said to David, 'Yahweh has also put away your sin. You will not die. However, because of this deed you have given great occasion to Yahweh's enemies to blaspheme, the child also who is born to you will surely die.' Nathan departed to his house. Yahweh struck the child that Uriah's wife bore to David, and it was very sick. David therefore begged God for the child; and David fasted, and went in, and lay all night on the ground. The elders of his house arose beside him, to raise him up from the earth; but he would not, and he didn't eat bread with them. On the seventh day, the child died. David's servants were afraid to tell him that the child was dead, for they said, 'Behold, while the child was yet alive, we spoke to him, and he didn't listen to our voice. How will he then harm himself, if we tell him that the child is dead?' But when David saw that his servants were whispering together, David perceived that the child was dead; and David said to his servants, 'Is the child dead?' They said, 'He is dead.' Then David arose from the earth, and washed, and anointed himself, and changed his clothing; and he came into Yahweh's house, and worshipped. Then he came to his own house; and when he requested, they set bread before him, and he ate. Then his servants said to him, 'What is this that you have done? You fasted and wept for the child while he was alive, but when the child was dead, you rose up and ate bread.' He said, 'While the child was yet alive, I fasted and wept, for I said, "Who knows whether Yahweh will not be gracious to me, that the child may live?" But now he is dead, why should I fast? Can I bring him back again? I will go to him, but he will not return to me.'"

David showed an inordinate amount of perseverance, understanding, and acceptance of a very painful situation. What a role model he was because he was able to get up and worship God after the death of his infant son. We too lost a child, and there is nothing more painful than that kind of loss. My husband and I were devastated, and I know that I could not have immediately gotten up and praised God after losing Maggie. Although she did not die, the baby we tried to adopt went back to her birth mother, and *Maggie Bruno* ceased to exist. We grieved for her like she had died, and it was very painful. It honestly took both of us a while to come to terms with our loss and get back to where we could worship God with our whole hearts again. David was a better parent (and Christian) than I was.

And that brings me to another point to ponder: is God still good and worthy of our praise if He answers no to our prayers? I know of some people who have prayed for a loved one to get well, and when their loved one died, these people turned their backs on God and refused to worship Him any longer. Doesn't God have a right to say no to us? We may not understand His reasoning at the time (or even in the future), but can we trust God enough to believe that His way is always best?

In 1 Kings 19:1–4, we read about the prophet Elijah and a time when God, thankfully, said no to his prayer. This passage says, "Ahab told Jezebel all that Elijah had done, and how he had killed all the prophets with the sword. Then Jezebel sent a messenger to Elijah, saying, 'So let the gods do to me, and more also, if I don't make your life as the life of one of them by tomorrow about this time!' When he saw that, he arose, and ran for his life, and came to Beersheba, which belongs to Judah, and left his servant there. But he himself went a day's journey into the wilderness, and came and sat down under a juniper tree. Then he requested for himself that he might die, and said, 'It is enough. Now, o Yahweh, take away my life; for I am not better than my fathers.'"

After these verses, we read that God came to Elijah in a still small voice, and basically in this voice, God told Elijah to quit pouting and get back to work. If God had taken Elijah's life as he had requested, Elijah might have missed out on the most exciting moment of his life. We read about this event in 2 Kings 2:11, which says, "As they continued on and talked, behold, a chariot of fire and horses of fire separated them, and Elijah went up by a whirlwind into heaven." Can you imagine having been a witness to that? It had to have been phenomenal! But if God had killed Elijah when he requested, Elijah would have missed out on this experience with God.

Scripture tells us that David also wanted to build the temple of the Lord. Because David was known as "a man after God's own heart" (Acts 13:22), I think that it probably is reasonable to assume that David prayed about this desire of his. In 1 Chronicles 22:6–10, we read, "Then he called for Solomon his son, and commanded him to build a house for Yahweh, the God of Israel. David said to Solomon his son, 'As for me, it was in my heart to build a house to the name of Yahweh my God. But Yahweh's word came to me, saying, "You have shed blood abundantly, and have made great wars. You shall not build a house to my name, because you have shed much blood on the earth in my sight. Behold, a son shall be born to you, who shall be a man of peace. I will give him rest from all his enemies all around; for his name shall be Solomon, and I will give peace and quietness to Israel in his days. He shall build a house for my name; and he will be my son, and I will be his father; and I will establish the throne of his kingdom over Israel forever."'"

David's desire was to build the temple of the Lord, but God told him no because he was a man of war and had shed much blood during many battles. The temple had to be built by a man of peace, and God promised David that that was what his son Solomon would be—a man of peace and the one who would build the temple of the Lord. (God seemed to say no to David frequently, didn't He?)

The apostle Paul was a great man of God, and it is OK to presume that as such, he probably prayed to God about everything in his life. Would you not agree with that statement? In the New Testament, we read of at least two occasions when the apostle Paul was told no by God in response to his evangelistic efforts. In the book of Acts 16:6–8, we read, "When they had gone through the region of Phrygia and Galatia, they were forbidden by the Holy Spirit to speak the word in Asia. When they had come opposite Mysia, they tried to go into Bithynia, but the Spirit didn't allow them. Passing by Mysia, they came down to Troas." Paul wanted to go to Asia twice, but the Holy Spirit told him no both times. When we pray, we must be still and listen to God's response.

Paul also tells of another time when God said no to his prayers, and this circumstance is a more familiar one. We read about it in 2 Corinthians 12:7–10, which says, "By reason of the exceeding greatness of the revelations, that I should not be exalted excessively, a thorn in the flesh was given to me; a messenger of Satan to torment me, that I should not be exalted excessively. Concerning this thing, I begged the Lord three times that it might depart from me. He has said to me, 'My grace is sufficient for you, for my power is made perfect in weakness. Most gladly therefore I will rather glory in my weaknesses, that the power of Christ may rest on me. Therefore I take pleasure in weaknesses, in injuries, in necessities, in persecutions, and in distresses, for Christ's sake. For when I am weak, then I am strong.'" We are not told what type of malady Paul's *thorn in the flesh* was, but obviously, it was enough to bother him because he asked the Lord three times to remove it.

The Bible teaches that we need to be persistent in prayer. Key verses about this include Colossians 4:2; Ephesians 6:18; Philippians 4:6; 1 Chronicles 16:11; and 1 Thessalonians 5:17. Despite our persistence, however, we must be willing to submit to the will of God like Paul.

The most obvious time God said no to a prayer request was when Jesus was praying in the garden of Gethsemane. Mark records this event in his Gospel, Mark 14:35–36, which says, "He went forward a little, and fell on the ground, and prayed that, if it were possible, the hour might pass away from him. He said, 'Abba, Father, all things are possible to you. Please remove this cup from me. However, not what I desire, but what you desire.'" We know, of course, that God's answer to Jesus's prayer had to be no and that Jesus ultimately went to the cross to die for our sins. If God could say no to His only begotten Son, why do we get upset when He says no to our prayers? If He could tell Jesus no, why can't He tell us no? Doesn't God have a right to say no to whoever He wants?

We must believe that God knows what is best for us, and even though we can't always understand why He says no to our prayers, we must take His no answer on faith. As parents, we hate to say no to our children, but sometimes it's for their own good. We can't give our children everything they want because sometimes they don't really know what they want, what they want isn't good for them, or they don't always view some things the way we as adults do. God, as our heavenly Father, sometimes says no to our prayers for the same reasons. And remember a point that we made in the previous chapter: sometimes God says no to what we think we want so that He can give us something even better!

THOUGHT QUESTIONS

1. Did you find King David's actions callous after the death of his son? What do you think about the fact that David was able to immediately get up and worship God after the loss of his child? Could you have done that in the same situation?

2. Can you think of other people in the Bible who prayed for something and God said no to their requests?

3. After studying this chapter, do you still think that God has a right to say no to any of our prayers? Why or why not?

4. Can you think of a time when you prayed for something, God said no to your prayer, but ended up giving you something better in the long run?

LESSON 9

Prayers That God Always Answers in the Affirmative

ARE THERE ANY PRAYERS TO WHICH GOD WILL ALWAYS SAY YES? I BELIEVE there are a few. We will look at some of these in this chapter.

First, if we submit ourselves to the Lord and pray for His will to be done in our lives, that is obviously a prayer that God will answer with a resounding yes. God wants us to show our dependence upon Him and our willingness to submit to His will in our lives. Not only can we pray for God to do His will in our lives, but we can also pray that God will reveal His will for our lives.

Psalm 143:10 says, "Teach me to do your will, for you are my God. Your Spirit is good. Lead me in the land of uprightness." The psalmist knew that God was willing to show what His good and perfect will was. Paul wrote in his epistle to the Philippians, "For it is God who works in you both to will and to work, for his good pleasure" (Philippians 2:13). John tells us in 1 John 2:17, "The world is passing away with its lusts, but he who does God's will remains forever." Ephesians 5:17 reads as follows, "Therefore don't be foolish, but understand what the will of the Lord is." These passages point out that it is possible for man to understand what the will of God is. Ephesians 6:6 says, "Not in the way of service only when eyes are on you, as men pleasers, but as servants of Christ, doing the will of God from the heart." We aren't to just pretend to be good Christians, trying to do the will of God when others are watching us, but we are to *show* that our intentions are to do God's will all the time because that is the desire in our hearts.

In addition to praying for God's will to be done in our lives, we can also pray for guidance from God in living our day-to-day lives. Genesis 24:12–27 tells of the time Abraham sent his servant back to Mesopotamia to find a wife for his son, Isaac. Wanting to be successful on his mission, the servant prayed to God for a specific sign as to which woman God had selected for Isaac, and verse 15 in this passage says, "Before he had finished speaking, behold, Rebekah came out, who was born to Bethuel the son of Milcah, the wife of Nahor, Abraham's brother, with her pitcher on her shoulder." She was the one God had selected for Isaac, and God granted the specific request of Abraham's servant to know which woman God had picked.

I too have made specific requests of God in the past, and when I'm trying to decide between two alternatives, my prayers have gone like this: "Dear God, if the outcome of this decision has a specific bearing on Your will for my life, if it matters to you at all, please make Your will so blatantly obvious to me that I cannot miss it." And He always has. When I couldn't decide if it was God's will for me to go to nursing school (even though I was really going to have to put myself in debt to do so and go to school while working a full-time job), I prayed that God would show me His will. I filed all the required paperwork in July even though it was very late to try to get into the fall semester of nursing school, and every one of my pieces of paperwork got approved on the last day of the deadline! To me, that was a definite yes from God. And I have never regretted this decision. (I had also asked advice from my minister at that time, Bill Hopkins, who was not only my minister but a father figure to me as well since I had lost my own father early in life. I will never forget what "Dad" said to me: "Well, look at it this way. If you go ahead and sign up for LPN [licensed practical nursing] school, in another year, you can be another year older and a nurse. Or in another year, if you don't go to nursing school, you can simply be another year older." Well, that definitely put things into perspective!)

And again, when I couldn't decide between which two nursing jobs to take, I prayed for God's will to be done and for Him to show me what it was. Well, one facility kept dawdling over processing my application, and the paperwork at the other facility went through without a hitch.

The second facility offered me a lot more money than the first facility eventually offered me too. That too was a no-brainer.

When we are praying for God's guidance, there are some scriptures that we can consider. Psalm 25:4-5 says, "Show me your ways, Yahweh. Teach me your paths. Guide me in your truth, and teach me. For you are the God of my salvation, I wait for you all day long." Verse 9 of this same Psalm says, "He will guide the humble in justice. He will teach the humble his way." Psalm 48:14 reads, "For this God is our God forever and ever. He will be our guide even to death." Submitting to God's guidance, however, means that we ultimately also submit to His divine will for our lives. Why shouldn't we? The God of heaven who can take the horrible death of His only Son Jesus and make something good out of it (eternal life for all who believe and obey His will) can surely be trusted with our futures!

Other verses that talk about guidance from God include Psalm 32:8, Psalm 73:24, Psalm 143:8, Isaiah 30:21, Isaiah 58:11, Jeremiah 10:23, 2 Thessalonians 3:5, and Galatians 5:18.

Many Bible verses tell us that God will give us His strength, comfort, and peace if we just pray. These verses include Joshua 1:9; Psalm 46:1–3, 55:22; Isaiah 41:10; Matthew 6:25–34; John 14:27; 2 Corinthians 12:9; 2 Thessalonians 3:16; and Philippians 4:6–7.

God will also answer when we sincerely pray for forgiveness of our sins. In 1 John 1:9, it reads, "If we confess our sins, he is faithful and righteous to forgive us the sins, and to cleanse us from all unrighteousness." These obviously would include sins of commission and omission. God is merciful to His children as we read in Psalm 86:5, which says, "For you, Lord, are good and ready to forgive; abundant in loving kindness to all who call on you." Not only should we pray for forgiveness of sins in general, but we need to be specific about our sins.

The Bible also tells us that we can ask for wisdom. James wrote in chapter 1 of his epistle, verse 5, "But if any of you lacks wisdom, let him ask of God, who gives to all liberally and without reproach, and it will be given to him." I don't think this is just any kind of wisdom, however. I think God blesses us when we ask for spiritual wisdom as Solomon did in 1 Kings 3:514: "In Gibeon, Yahweh appeared to Solomon in a dream by night; and God said, 'Ask for what I should give you.' Solomon said, 'You have shown to your servant David my father great loving kindness, because he walked before you in truth, in righteousness, and in uprightness of heart with you. You have kept for him this great loving kindness, that you have given him a son to sit on his throne, as it is today. Now, Yahweh my God, you have made your servant king instead of David my father. I am just a little child. I don't know how to go out or come in. Your servant is among your people which you have chosen, a great people, that can't be numbered or counted for multitude. Give your servant therefore an understanding heart to judge your people, that I may discern between good and evil, for who is able to judge this great people of yours?' This request pleased the Lord, that Solomon had asked this thing. God said to him, 'Because you have asked this thing, and have not asked for yourself long life, nor have you asked for riches for yourself, nor have you asked for the life of your enemies, but have asked for yourself understanding to discern justice; behold, I have done according to your word. Behold, I have given you a wise and understanding heart; so that there has been no one like you before you, and after you none will arise like you. I have also given you that which you have not asked, both riches and honor, so that there will not be any among the kings like you for all your days. If you will walk in my ways, to keep my statutes and my commandments, as your father David walked, then I will lengthen your days.'"

Because Solomon did not selfishly ask for riches and honor but wisdom to lead God's people (spiritual wisdom), God granted him all three. This is another example of God giving His children more than that for which they asked.

I also think that God will bless our evangelistic efforts if we pray and ask Him to do so. After all, Matthew 28:18–20, which is sometimes called the Great Commission by Christians, says, "Jesus came to them and spoke to them, saying, 'All authority has been given to me in heaven and on earth. Go and make disciples of all nations, baptizing them in the name of the Father and of the Son and of the Holy Spirit, teaching them to observe all things that I commanded you. Behold, I am with you always, even to the end of the age. Amen.'" When considering the Great Commission, we need to be aware that our sole duty is to spread the Gospel. The outcome is up to the individual and God.

After all, God did as Jabez requested in 1 Chronicles 4:10 (NIV) when Jabez asked the Lord to "enlarge my territory." *Territory* here refers to the spiritual influence of Jabez, not a physical territory. The latter part of this verse says, "God granted him that which he requested."

We can pray for boldness as Paul asked the saints in Ephesus to pray for his boldness in proclaiming the Gospel of Christ. In his book, Paul wrote, "With all prayer and requests, praying at all times in the Spirit, and being watchful to this end in all perseverance and requests for all the saints: on my behalf, that utterance may be given to me in opening my mouth, to make known with boldness the mystery of the Good News, for which I am an ambassador in chains, that in it I may speak boldly, as I ought to speak" (Ephesians 6:18–20). Many of us desire boldness to speak to others about Christ. Unfortunately, we think that we must be eloquent and articulate when all we must do is simply share what Jesus Christ has done for us in our own lives. Our message doesn't have to be complicated or elaborate; it just needs to be sincere and honest.

We also need to pray for opportunities to share the Gospel with others. Paul wrote in his epistle to the Colossians 4:3–4, "Praying together for us also, that God may open to us a door for the word, to speak the mystery of Christ, for which I am also in bonds, that I may reveal it as I ought to speak." If God wants us to share the Gospel with those around us, why, then, wouldn't He give us the words, courage, and eloquence needed to do so?

We need to pray for our friends and families to come to Jesus before it is too late. The older I get, the more urgently I sense this. We can pray for those close to us to realize that as Paul wrote in 1 Corinthians 3:6–7, "I planted. Apollos watered. But God gave the increase. So then neither he who plants is anything, nor he who waters, but God who gives the increase." All we must do is plant the seed and leave the rest to God. Whether an individual chooses to obey the Gospel is up to him or her.

Many times, I have prayed for friends or family members to simply open their hearts to God. I have a dear friend in the Memphis area for whom I have been praying that God would open her heart to Him. About a year ago, when my husband and I were visiting my friend and her husband, I had a sudden impulse to say to her, "You know, I don't understand why people who choose to ignore God in this life and not go to church or read His Word or pray or spend any time here on earth with God think that they will be spending time with God in eternity? If they don't want to spend time with God here, why would they want to do it in heaven?" (One of our ministers, Mike, likes to call these people *practical atheists*, meaning that they *say* that they believe in God, but they live like He has no bearing on their lives.) Anyway, less than a month later, my friend told me that she had begun studying the Bible with the preacher's wife who lived next door! If we don't feel that the time is right to approach our friends and family members about their eternal destiny, we can at least pray that God opens their hearts to Him.

We also need to pray for more people to evangelize the world. Luke 10:2 says, "The harvest is indeed plentiful, but the laborers are few. Pray therefore to the Lord of the harvest, that he may send out laborers into his harvest." (Matthew 9:38 echoes this same sentiment.) Time is of the essence. It seems as if each year that passes finds fewer and fewer people who identify as "Christians." We must continue to evangelize the world before Christianity dies out altogether. This is, indeed, a prayer that God will say yes to.

God will answer if we pray for strength for the days ahead. Luke 21:36 (NIV) says, "Be always on the watch, and pray that you may be able to escape all that is about to happen, and that you may be able to stand before the Son of Man." Praying for strength for our day shows our dependence upon God.

Second Peter 3:9 sums it all up when Peter wrote, "The Lord is not slow concerning his promise, as some count slowness; but he is patient with us, not wanting that anyone should perish, but that all should come to repentance." We should fervently pray that all non-Christians come to Jesus before it is eternally too late.

THOUGHT QUESTIONS

1. What are some things for which we can pray that God will always grant us?

2. Is there anything else that you can think of for which we can pray and that God will always answer with a yes?

3. Is there someone you can think of right now with whom you need to be sharing the Gospel? Will you begin today praying that God will open that person's heart to His message?

LESSON 10

Sometimes God's Answers to Prayers Were Immediate in the Bible

THE BIBLE GIVES US SOME EXAMPLES OF PEOPLE WHO PRAYED TO GOD and who received immediate answers to their prayers. One of the first of these people who comes to mind is the patriarch, Abraham. Obviously, we all know the story of how Abraham and Sarah waited years, even to their old age, in fact, before they received the son promised to them by God. But there was another time Abraham prayed to God and God's answer came almost immediately. This story is told in the book of Genesis 20:17–18, which says, "Abraham prayed to God. God healed Abimelech and his wife, and his female servants, and they bore children For Yahweh had closed up tight all the wombs of the house of Abimelech, because of Sarah, Abraham's wife." Now, did all these women immediately become pregnant at the same time? Not necessarily, but because of Abraham's prayer, they all regained the *ability to have* children again when God opened their wombs.

In the book of Numbers 12:10–15, we read of a time in the life of Moses when God answered Moses's prayer immediately, but the result occurred a week later. These verses say, "The cloud departed from over the Tent; and behold, Miriam was leprous, as white as snow. Aaron said to Moses, 'Oh, my lord, please don't count this sin against us, in which we have done foolishly, and in which we have sinned. Let her not, I pray, be as one dead, of whom the flesh is half-consumed when he comes out of his mother's womb.' Moses cried to Yahweh, saying, 'Heal her, God,

I beg you!' Yahweh said to Moses, 'If her father had but spit in her face, shouldn't she be ashamed seven days? Let her be shut up outside the camp seven days, and after that she shall be brought in again.' Miriam was shut up outside the camp seven days, and the people didn't travel until Miriam was brought in again. Afterward the people traveled from Hazeroth, and encamped in the wilderness of Paran." Miriam had to pay the consequences for her jealousy of Moses and her speaking out against him. While God agreed to heal Miriam, she still had to wait the customary seven days of purification and restoration.

Samson was a man who got off to a good start and then took a wrong turn somewhere. His parents were apparently devout believers, whose son was promised to them by an angel of God. After the angel's visit, Samson's father, Manoah, asked the angel to return and tell them how to raise their son. (See Judges 13:2–25.) Samson was also destined by God to save His people from the Philistines. But Samson fell in love with a pagan woman from Timnah, and that's when his downfall started. God had told His people not to intermarry with the Canaanites, and Samson disobeyed God's explicit command. Not only was Samson an Israelite but his parents had set also him apart as a Nazirite since birth, meaning that he was to serve the Lord all of his days. Later, Samson fell in love with another woman, Delilah, who was probably a Philistine and may have even been a temple prostitute. She brought about the downfall of Samson, who spent the last years of his life blind and grinding grain in prison. Although it would seem like God had forgotten such a disobedient man, the Bible tells us that when Samson prayed his last prayer, God was there.

In the book of Judges 16, we read of the death of Samson. Verses 25–30 say, "When their hearts were merry, they said, 'Call for Samson that he may entertain us.' They called for Samson out of the prison; and he performed before them. They set him between the pillars; and Samson said to the boy who held him by the hand, 'Allow me to feel the pillars whereupon the house rests, that I may lean on them.' Now the house was full of men and women, who saw while Samson performed. Samson called to Yahweh, and said, 'Lord Yahweh, remember me, please, and strengthen me, please, only this once, God, that I may be at once avenged of the Philistines for my two eyes.' Samson took hold of the middle two pillars on which the house rested, and leaned on them, the one with his right hand, and the other with his left. Samson said, 'Let me die with the Philistines!' He bowed himself with all his might; and the house fell on the lords, and all the people who were therein. So the dead that he killed at his death were more than those he killed in his life." Despite his sinful life, God answered Samson's last prayer at the end of his life, and Samson is even mentioned in the "Hall of Faith" (Hebrews 11:32). God's answer to the prayer of Samson was immediate and complete, and God used Samson to kill many of the wicked Philistines.

Many times, God gave immediate answers to His prophets, especially when they were trying to bring someone back from the dead. One such example is found in 1 Kings 17:17–24 when we read of a time when God immediately answered the prayer of His prophet, Elijah. In this passage, we read, "After these things, the son of the woman, the mistress of the house, became sick; and his sickness was so severe that there was no breath left in him. She said to Elijah, 'What have I to do with you, you man of God? You have come to me to bring my sin to memory, and to kill my son!' He said to her, 'Give me your son.' He took him out of her bosom and carried him up to the room where he stayed and laid him on his own bed. He cried to Yahweh, and said, 'Yahweh my God, have you also brought evil on the widow with whom I am staying, by killing her son?' He stretched himself on the child three times, and cried to Yahweh, and said again, 'Yahweh my God, please let this child's soul come into him again.' Yahweh listened to the voice of Elijah, and the soul of the child came into him again, and he revived. Elijah took the child, and brought him down out of the room and into the house, and delivered him to his mother; and Elijah said, 'Behold, your son lives.' The woman said to Elijah, 'Now I know that you are a man of God, and that Yahweh's word in your mouth is truth.'

Other people who prayed to God and God allowed them to raise someone from the dead include the prophet Elisha in 2 Kings 4:18–37; the apostle Peter in Acts 9:36–42; Paul in Acts 20:7–12; and of course, Jesus Himself as recounted in the book of Luke 7:11–17; 8:49–56; and John 11:1–44.

We read of another immediate answered prayer in 1 Chronicles 5:18–20, which tells us, "The sons of Reuben, the Gadites, and the half-tribe of Manasseh, of valiant men, men able to bear buckler and sword, and to shoot with bow, and skillful in war, were forty-four thousand seven hundred sixty, that were able to go out to war. They made war with the Hagrites, with Jetur, and Naphish, and Nodab. They were helped against them, and the Hagrites were delivered into their hand, and all who were with them, for they cried to God in the battle, and he answered them, because they put their trust in him."

Other passages where God's people were in battle and prayed to God for deliverance and their prayers were answered include 2 Chronicles 20:2–30; 32:1–22; and 1 Samuel 23:2–29.

In 2 Kings 6:15–17, we read of a time when the prophet Elisha prayed for his servant. These verses say, "When the servant of the man of God had risen early, and gone out, behold, an army with horses and chariots was around the city. His servant said to him, 'Alas, my master! What shall we do?' He answered, 'Don't be afraid; for those who are with us are more than those who are with them.' Elisha prayed, and said, 'Yahweh, please open his eyes that he may see.' Yahweh opened the young man's eyes; and he saw: and behold, the mountain was full of horses and chariots of fire around Elisha."

Other examples of God's immediate answers to prayers can be found in 1 Samuel 30:1–8; 2 Kings 19:14–19, 35–36; Daniel 2:17–23; Acts 4:20–31, 12:1–17, and 16:25–27.

Isaiah 65:24 even tells us that sometimes God will answer our prayers before we even finish praying! I witnessed this happen firsthand when a close friend of ours died of cancer.

Roseanna was a vibrant, outgoing, talkative woman who had just recently given her life to Christ and had been baptized. Rose was a beautiful friend, both inside and out. Four years before her death, it was discovered that she had inherited the BRCA1 gene. Now she was facing the daunting prospect of fighting both stage 4 ovarian cancer and stage 3 breast cancer at the same time. Through it all, Rose only cried once (when told of her diagnosis) and literally never complained nor questioned God. She was a trooper throughout the entire ordeal. But the end of the road had come for Rose, and she knew it. The cancer had metastasized to both her liver and her large intestine, and she was facing surgery. Without the surgery, the doctors told her that her colon would rupture and she would surely die. With the surgery, her chances of survival were 5 percent at best, not very good odds, to say the least.

Rose decided to have the surgery. Immediately afterward, she was taken to ICU, where she continued to decline. Her husband's family was called in (Rose had already lost both of her parents and her younger brother years before) as were her close friends. The decision was made that there was nothing more that could be done, and Rose was moved from ICU to a regular hospital bed. All of us gathered around.

Finally, Lee Ann, Rose's sister-in-law, asked her uncle Max to pray for Rose. We all joined hands around Rose's bed. By this time, she was fully unresponsive. At first, Uncle Max prayed for comfort and healing for Rose, but suddenly, his tone switched and he began to pray aloud that if it wasn't God's will for Rose to get better, God "would send an army of angels to conduct Rose's soul into heaven right then that very minute."

I was standing near the head of Rose's bed toward one side. My husband was standing at the other side, toward the foot of the bed. As Uncle Max continued with his heartfelt prayer, I sensed a change in Rose's breathing. As a nurse of many years, I recognized that change. I opened my eyes to peer at Rose, and what I saw caused my heart to skip a beat. She was suddenly breathing the erratic pattern that signaled impending death. Up until that moment, there was nothing in Rose's condition that indicated that she couldn't have easily lasted another day or two before passing. But as Uncle Max prayed on, it became obvious to me that Rose was literally and actively dying in front of my eyes. Please understand that all of this occurred in the space of just a couple of minutes although telling it makes it seem much longer.

I glanced up and saw my husband looking at me with a puzzled look on his face. Everyone else still had their eyes closed, praying. I mouthed out to Rick, "She's going now," and his expression changed to one of shock.

As Max prayed his final "amen," Roseanna took her last breath and peacefully died. As everyone raised their heads, they saw me checking her carotid pulse. I looked across the bed at Lee Ann and asked her to get the nurse. Roseanna's husband, Greg, asked me if Rose was gone, and I nodded my head.

Everyone in that room was stunned at the suddenness of Rose's death. Although we knew that she was not going to survive, nothing had indicated to the doctors, nurses, or any of us that her death was imminent. All of us were convinced that God had decided to answer Uncle Max's prayer immediately and take Rose's soul to heaven. Even today, remembering this incident fills me with a sense of awe and amazement at how God chose to immediately answer Uncle Max's prayer. One minute, Rose was lying there, looking like she could easily have lasted another day or so, and the next minute, she was gone.

In this chapter, we studied times when God's answers to His people's prayers were immediate. In the next chapter, we will study when God's people had to wait years for God's answers to their prayers and what we can learn from their circumstances.

THOUGHT QUESTIONS

1. Has God ever answered one of your prayers almost immediately? Did that response serve to bolster your faith in Him?

2. Why do you suppose God chooses to answer some prayers rather quickly, and at other times, He makes His people wait for years before He answers their prayers? Do you think that at times, circumstances necessitate a faster response from God? Why or why not?

3. Can you think of anyone else in the Bible who prayed to God and received an immediate answer?

4. What do you think of my story of my friend Rose and her sudden death?

LESSON 11

Sometimes God's Answers to Prayers Didn't Come for Years

THE BIBLE TELLS OF SEVERAL PEOPLE WHO WAITED YEARS FOR GOD TO answer their prayers. This chapter will examine some of these people and how long they had to wait on God.

One point that we need to remember is that just because you have to wait for an answer from God does not mean that God doesn't hear your prayer or doesn't care. Sometimes waiting is part of God's plan. There are lessons to be learned by waiting, and we will examine these later.

Abraham, the great patriarch, was told by God in the book of Genesis 15:13–16, "He said to Abram, 'Know for sure that your offspring will live as foreigners in a land that is not theirs, and will serve them. They will afflict them four hundred years. I will also judge that nation, whom they will serve. Afterward they will come out with great wealth, but you will go to your fathers in peace. You will be buried at a good old age. In the fourth generation they will come here again, for the iniquity of the Amorite is not yet full.'"

In the book of Exodus 2:23–25, we read, "In the course of those many days, the king of Egypt died, and the children of Israel sighed because of the bondage, and they cried, and their cry came up to God because of the bondage. God heard their groaning, and God remembered the covenant with Abraham, with Isaac, and with Jacob. God saw the children of Israel, and God was concerned about them."

Then Exodus 12:40 says that it all came to pass as God had said: "Now the time that the children of Israel lived in Egypt was four hundred thirty years. At the end of four hundred thirty years, to the day, all of Yahweh's armies went out from the land of Egypt." Can you imagine that *over four hundred years passed* before God answered the prayers of the Israelite people? It goes without saying that the people who were alive when God made this promise to Abraham didn't live to see the promised land or the end of their slavery. (It is also interesting to note that four hundred years passed between the end of the Old Testament and the beginning of the New Testament and the coming of the long-promised Messiah. Four hundred years has great significance in the Bible.)

Another example of someone who waited on the completion of a promise from God was Isaac. In the book of Genesis 25:20–21, we read, "Isaac was forty years old when he took Rebekah the daughter of Bethuel the Syrian of Paddan Aram, the sister of Laban the Syrian, to be his wife. Isaac entreated Yahweh for his wife, because she was barren. Yahweh was entreated by him, and Rebekah his wife conceived." But the Bible also tells us that God's answer to Isaac's prayer was not immediate because further in that same chapter in the book of Genesis, in the latter part of verse 26, it says, "Isaac was sixty years old when she bore them [Jacob and Esau]." The Lord did not answer the prayer of Isaac for nineteen years!

Another woman in the Bible who prayed and had to wait years to become pregnant was Rachel, the wife of Jacob. Genesis 30:22–23 says, "God remembered Rachel, and God listened to her, and opened her womb. She conceived, bore a son, and said, 'God has taken away my reproach.'" This occurred after her sister Leah, who had also married Jacob, had given birth to six sons and one daughter. Rachel's handmaid Bilhah had given birth to two sons with Jacob, and Leah's handmaid Zilpah had also given birth to two sons with Jacob. Poor Rachel had had to wait *years* for the birth of her firstborn child, Joseph.

The book of Genesis tells us more about Joseph and how he had to wait on God's timing in his life. In Genesis 37:2, we read, "This is the story of the generations of Jacob. Joseph, being seventeen years old, was feeding the flock with his brothers." Verses 5– 8 of this same chapter say, "Joseph dreamed a dream, and he told it to his brothers, and they hated him all the more. He said to them, 'Please hear this dream which I have dreamed: for behold, we were binding sheaves in the field, and behold, my sheaf arose and also stood upright; and behold, your sheaves came around, and bowed down to my sheaf.' His brothers asked him, 'Will you indeed reign over us? Will you indeed have dominion over us?' They hated him all the more for his dreams and for his words." Verse 28 of this chapter continues the story of Joseph and says, "Midianites who were merchants passed by, and they drew and lifted Joseph out of the pit, and sold Joseph to the Ishmaelites for twenty pieces of silver. The merchants brought Joseph into Egypt."

Later, the book of Genesis tells us in chapter 41:46 that "Joseph was thirty years old when he stood before Pharaoh king of Egypt. Joseph went out from the presence of Pharaoh, and went throughout all the land of Egypt." Although no prayers of Joseph are recorded in the book of Genesis, the hand of God is obvious in the life of this young man. Don't you suppose Joseph did a lot of praying when he was taken from his family, sold into slavery, and taken away to Egypt? I know that I would have been praying continually for rescue from this situation! But God had plans for Joseph, and they eventually came to pass. Joseph waited thirteen years to see the realization of his youthful dreams, but God was with him while he waited.

In Deuteronomy 3:2, we read, "This is because both of you (Moses and Aaron) broke faith with me in the presence of the Israelites at the waters of Meribah Kadesh in the desert of Zin and because you did not uphold my holiness among the Israelites. Therefore, you will see the land only from a distance; you will not enter the land I am giving to the people of Israel." This punishment was not only because Moses struck the rock when God told him to speak to it (Numbers 20:8–12), but because Moses also said at that time, "Listen, you rebels, must *we* bring you water out of this rock?" By saying this, Moses was taking part of the credit from God for providing water for the people from the rock.

What does this story of Moses have to do with prayer and waiting? Just this: Moses waited many years to finally enter the promised land, which is recorded in the book of Matthew 17:1–3, which says, "After six days, Jesus took with him Peter, James and John his brother and brought them up into a high mountain by themselves. He was transfigured before them. His face shone like the sun, and his garments became as white as the light. Behold, Moses and Elijah appeared to them talking with him." Moses waited approximately a thousand years or so to finally put his feet down in the promised land!

Hannah was another woman in the Bible who prayed for a baby and waited years for God to answer her prayers. (There seemed to be several women who prayed for babies in the Bible, didn't there? I can truly relate to these women after having to have a hysterectomy at the young age of twenty-five due to health issues. I, too, longed for a baby but knew that mine would have to be adopted.) In 1 Samuel 1:1–20, we read Hannah's story. Specifically verses 1–3 of this chapter say, "Now there was a certain man of Ramathaim Sophim, of the hill country of Ephraim, and his name was Elkanah, the son of Jeroham, the son of Elihu, the son of Tohu, the son of Zuph, an Ephramite. He had two wives. The name of one was Hannah, and the name of the other Peninnah. Peninnah had children, but Hannah had no children. This man went out of his city from year to year to worship and to sacrifice to Yahweh of Amies in Shiloh." Verses 6–7 of this same chapter add more to the story, "Her [Hannah's] rival provoked her severely, to irritate her, because Yahweh had shut up her womb. So year by year, when she went up to Yahweh's house, her rival provoked her. Therefore she wept, and didn't eat." Each year, Hannah went to the house of the Lord with her husband, Elkanah, and prayed earnestly for a child. And every year, she went home and found that once again, her prayers had not been answered. How discouraging it must have been for her! It's hard enough for a woman to want to conceive and be unable to, but then to have what the Bible describes as *her rival* rubbing her nose in it must have been nearly intolerable!

One time, as Hannah accompanied her husband to the temple, the priest Eli saw her praying silently to the Lord and thought that she was drunk. Hannah explained that she had merely been pouring out her soul to the Lord. Something in her countenance probably made Eli realize the earnestness of her prayers because the Bible tells us in verse 17 that the priest said to her, "Go in peace, and may the God of Israel grant your petition that you have asked of him." Verses 19–20 say, "They rose up in the morning early and worshipped Yahweh, then returned and came to their house in Ramah. Then Elkanah knew Hannah his wife, and Yahweh remembered her. When the time had come, Hannah conceived, and bore a son; and she named him Samuel, saying, 'Because I have asked him of Yahweh.'"

David, the man of God, had to wait years before becoming king of Israel. As a man of God, don't you suppose David prayed about this daily?

First Samuel 16:1–13 tells us that David was a young man when he was anointed by Samuel to be king. But it's not until 2 Samuel 2–4 that we are told that David was a young married man with two wives when he became king over the house of Judah, and 2 Samuel 5:4 says that David was thirty years old when he became king over all of Israel.

In the book of Daniel, we learn that Daniel prayed to God and his prayer was heard, but God's response was delayed. We read of this incident in Daniel 10:12–14, which says, "Then he said to me, 'Don't be afraid, Daniel, for from the first day that you set your heart to understand, and to humble yourself before your God, your words were heard. I have come for your words' sake. But the prince of the kingdom of Persia withstood me twenty-one days, but, behold, Michael, one of the chief princes, came to help me because I remained there with the kings of Persia. Now I have come to make you understand what will happen to your people in the latter days, for the vision is yet for many days.'" God's answer to Daniel was delayed for three weeks. Do you think that perhaps Daniel wondered if he was ever going to get an answer from God? Or did he automatically assume that God's answer was a no?

In the New Testament, we read of a priest named Zacharias who had prayed for years for a child. The first part of chapter 1 of the book of Luke is devoted to the story of Zacharias. Verses 5–7 tell us, "There was in the days of Herod, the king of Judea, a certain priest named Zacharias, of the priestly division of Abijah. He had a wife of the daughters of Aaron, and her name was Elizabeth. They were both righteous before God, walking blamelessly in all the commandments and ordinances of the Lord. But they had no child, because Elizabeth was barren, and they were both well advanced in years."

We read on in this same chapter and learn that while Zacharias was performing his priestly duties, an angel appeared to him. Luke 1:13–14 says, "But the angel said to him, 'Don't be afraid, Zacharias, because your request has been heard, and your wife, Elizabeth, will bear you a son, and you shall call his name John. You will have joy and gladness, and many will rejoice at his birth.'" True to the angel's words, Elizabeth did indeed give birth to a son in her old age, and he was John the Baptist. How many years do you suppose Zacharias and Elizabeth had been praying for a child? As they started getting older and older, don't you think that it would have felt like it was time to give up on that dream? Did they continue to believe that anything was possible with God, considering how old Abraham and Sarah were when they had Isaac (Genesis 17 and 21), or did they start to believe that they were past their prime and maybe were not worthy of the same blessing God had given Abraham and Sarah? The point of this story is, though, that Zacharias and Elizabeth prayed for a son for years and God didn't answer their prayers until they were very old. The birth of John the Baptist was almost as great a miracle as the birth of Jesus!

The book of Luke 2:25–31 also tells us, "Behold, there was a man in Jerusalem whose name was Simeon. This man was righteous and devout, looking for the consolation of Israel, and the Holy Spirit was on him. It had been revealed to him by the Holy Spirit that he should not see death before he had seen the Lord's Christ. He came in the Spirit into the temple. When the parents brought in the child, Jesus, that they might do concerning him according to the custom of the law, then he received him into his arms, and blessed God, and said, 'Now you are releasing your servant, Master, according to your word, in peace; for my eyes have seen your salvation, which you have prepared before the face of all peoples; a light for revelation to the nations, and the glory of your people Israel." Isn't it interesting that the Holy Spirit, who hadn't yet been given to Christians (not until the day of Pentecost in the book of Acts 2:1–3), was active in the life of this man who had seemingly spent his life looking forward to the coming Messiah? What a promise to receive, that he would not die until he had looked upon the Savior of the world! We, who are Christians, have the assurance that when we pray, God hears us. This is an equally wonderful promise: to have immediate access to the Creator of the world and the Lord of hosts. Do we look at it the same way? Do we acknowledge that God is not only our Father but our Savior too?

The apostle John tells us in chapter 11 of his book about the illness of Lazarus and how Jesus deliberately delayed coming to Lazarus's sisters Mary and Martha until Lazarus had already been dead for four days. Verse 3 of this chapter tells us that Mary and Martha sent word to Jesus that Lazarus was very sick. These women were devout followers of Jesus. They believed him to be the Messiah. They knew of His great deeds of healing the sick. They had heard how He caused the blind to see, the lame to walk, the dumb to speak, and the deaf to hear. They knew that all things were possible with Jesus. Don't you know that they were praying mightily that Jesus would arrive in time to heal their beloved brother, Lazarus?

But verse 6 of this same chapter tells us, "When therefore he heard that he was sick, he stayed two days in the place where he was." Why would Jesus, who claimed to love these friends of his, do such a thing? Why didn't he rush to Mary and Martha's sides? Verse 14 goes on to reveal why Jesus delayed going to his friend's sick bed. It says, "So Jesus said to them plainly then, 'Lazarus is dead. I am glad for your sakes that I was not there, so that you may believe. Nevertheless, let's go to him.'" As Jesus had told His disciples, Lazarus was dead when they arrived, and according to his sister Martha, he had already been buried for four days (v. 39). Verses 41–44 tell us, "So they took away the stone from the place where the dead man was lying. Jesus lifted up his eyes and said, 'Father, I thank you that you listened to me. I know that you always listen to me, but because of the multitude standing around I said this, that they may believe that you sent me.' When he had said this, he cried with a loud voice, 'Lazarus, come out!' He who was dead came out, bound hand and foot with wrappings, and his face was wrapped around with a cloth. Jesus said to them, 'Free him and let him go.'"

Four days really doesn't seem like such a long time for Mary and Martha to wait for Jesus to come to them compared to some of the other people we have studied who waited years for the answers to their prayers, but after Lazarus died, don't you suppose that they probably just gave up on the idea of seeing their brother again in this life? But Jesus had a purpose in allowing Lazarus to die before he traveled to Bethany, and that purpose was so that he could raise Lazarus to life in front of his apostles and cement their faith in Him. This teaches us that many times God has a purpose in delaying the answer to our prayers, and we must trust that He knows best what we need.

Whether it was a short wait or a long one, the answers to these people's prayers were not immediate. And like us, they didn't know if they were going to be waiting days or years for an answer from God. Delayed answers from God may seem like refusals at the time, but perhaps God wants to show us that the time is not right yet for what we want to happen. Perhaps He is testing our faith—and our patience. We need to learn to trust God's infinite wisdom and timing.

Waiting is hard. No one in this world seems to want to wait anymore. All of life seems to be rush, rush, rush. Instant coffee. Instant connections to others through social media. Express lanes to check out groceries. In less than a minute, a fax can be sent to someone in another part of the building, another state, or another part of the world. Is it any wonder that sometimes we find it difficult to wait for God to answer our prayers? What if you knew beforehand that you were going to have to wait *years* for the answer to one of your deepest desires, to one of your most heartfelt prayers? Could you do it? Could you be patient and remain faithful?

I can relate to this! When we tried to adopt our daughter, Maggie, she was only two weeks old. She was ours for a total of 278 days. When we had to return her to her birth mother just before her first birthday, my husband, I, and our families were devastated. I knew in my heart that her birth mother wouldn't allow me to look her up until her eighteenth birthday, if then. When we first lost her, I counted the days without her. I focused on all the things I was missing with her—birthdays, being a toddler, school days, etc. Daily, I was filled with despair. I thought about her all the time. Was she cold? Was she hungry? Was she loved? I used to think that the worst thing that could happen to a mother, any mother, would be for her child to disappear and for the mother to never know what happened to him or her. I was living this nightmare. I knew that Maggie had gone back to a less-than-desirable home life and one without God in the home, and I grieved for her.

But God works in mysterious ways (and in ways that we could never understand), and over the years, Maggie's mother died suddenly at a very young age, her biological father was sent to prison for life for sexually abusing Maggie, and my husband and I were able to reconnect with our daughter when she was thirteen years old—five years earlier than we had anticipated. Maggie is in counseling now to deal with the neglect, abuse, and horrific life she lived after being returned to her birth mother. The court system failed "Maggie," but God never left her or forsook her or us, and for that I am grateful. I still struggle with the thoughts of what our beautiful baby girl had to endure after she was returned to her birth parents before our adoption could be completed, but sometimes faith is simply accepting what is and trying not to be angry about it. Sometimes faith is simply letting go of the anger.

The book of Revelation 6:9–11 says, "When he opened the fifth seal, I saw underneath the altar the souls of those who had been killed for the Word of God, and for the testimony of the Lamb which they had. They cried with a loud voice, saying, 'How long, Master, the holy and true, until you judge and avenge our blood on those who dwell on the earth?' A long white robe was given to each of them. They were told that they should rest yet for a while, until their fellow servants and their brothers, who would also be killed even as they were, should complete their course." This tells me that even the martyred saints can grow impatient waiting for the vengeance of their deaths.

When God delays His answer to our prayers, do you think that He might possibly be waiting to see how we handle disappointment? Will we lose faith in Him? Will we become discouraged and give up? Or will we continue to trust Him and honor Him by our actions and not become bitter and disillusioned? Those of us who believe in God know that we will have to wait years to finally see once again the loved ones who have gone on before us, but it will be so worth the wait! Good things do come to those who wait!

THOUGHT QUESTIONS

1. Why do you think God waited until Abraham was one hundred years old and Sarah was ninety years old before He allowed them to have the son He had promised them? What was the purpose of their having to wait until they were past their childbearing years before Sarah became pregnant?

2. Have you ever had to wait years for God to answer a prayer of yours? Did you get discouraged while waiting? What did you do to fight the discouragement?

3. Why do you suppose God chooses to answer some prayers rather quickly and at other times to make His followers wait for years for an answer to their prayers?

4. The Bible teaches us in Ecclesiastes 3:1 that "for everything there is a season, and a time for every purpose under heaven." Could this be one reason God delays answering our prayers? What could His purpose be in making us wait?

5. Does waiting for a reply from God ever feel like a refusal?

LESSON 12

Not Waiting on God Can Lead to Sin

PRAYER IS MORE THAN JUST SIMPLY ASKING GOD FOR WHAT WE WANT. Prayer is waiting and listening for God's answers and directions for our lives.

What happens when you pray and pray for someone or about something and it seems like God is silent? Does He hear you? Does He care? It is so easy to become impatient at what seems to be God's lack of speed in answering our prayers. Many times, we find ourselves falling into a trap of self-pity, believing that God really doesn't care about what happens to us.

How many times do we become anxious about a situation, unwilling to wait for God to act, and so we take it upon ourselves to bring about the solution to our dilemma, only to find out in the end that we have made a royal mess of everything and then we must ask God to bail us out of the predicament of our own creation? The Bible is full of people who grew impatient with God and then had to deal with the consequences of trying to force God's hand in various situations. Let us see what we can learn from them.

But first, an admonition: Philippians 4:13 says, "I can do all things through Christ, who strengthens me." Please notice two things about this verse: (1) "I *can* do all things" (emphasis mine)—it's not that we *must* do all things, but that we *can* do all things and (2) "through Christ," which means that there are things that we can trust God to do without our interference and everything that is done must be in keeping with His will.

When struggling with impatience over a situation, we need to keep in mind who God is. God admonished Job in Job 38:4, "Where were you when I laid the foundations of the earth? Declare, if you have understanding." God created the entire universe without anyone's help, and He can handle our problems too if we will just get out of His way and trust His timing. Easier said than done, though, right? Sometimes we feel if we could just "help" God a little …

In Genesis 12:1–4, we read that God made a promise to a man named Abram. These verses say, "Now Yahweh said to Abram, 'Leave your country, and your relatives, and your father's house, and go to the land that I will show you. I will make of you a great nation. I will bless you and make your name great. You will be a blessing. I will bless those who bless you, and I will curse him who treats you with contempt. All the families of the earth will be blessed through you.' So Abram went, as Yahweh had told him. Lot went with him. Abram was seventy-five years old when he departed from Haran." Please note here that Abram was seventy-five years old when God first made the promise of a son to him.

Verses 6–7 of this same chapter say that God promised Abram that he would have children and that they would occupy the land of Canaan.

In Genesis 15:1–6, God became even more specific about His promise to Abram. These verses say, "After these things Yahweh's word came to Abram in a vision, saying, 'Don't be afraid, Abram. I am your shield, your exceedingly great reward.' Abram said, 'Lord Yahweh, what will you give me since I go childless, and he who will inherit my estate is Eliezer of Damascus?' Abram said, 'Behold, you have given no children to me: and behold, one born in my house is my heir.' Behold, Yahweh's word came to him, saying, 'This man will not be your heir, but he who will come out of your own body will be your heir.' Yahweh brought him outside, and said, 'Look now toward the sky, and count the stars if you are able to count them.' He said to Abram, 'So your offspring will be.' He believed in Yahweh, who credited it to him for righteousness." Notice here that Abram is starting to doubt God's promise to him since he and Sarai are getting older, yet they still have no son. Despite all that, Abram is trying to hold on to his faith!

But Abram's wife Sarai grew impatient and decided to put her own plan into action. Genesis 16:1–6 says, "Now Sarai, Abram's wife, bore him no children. She had a servant, an Egyptian, whose name was Hagar. Sarai said to Abram, 'See now, Yahweh has restrained me from bearing. Please go in to my servant. It may be that I will obtain children by her.' Abram listened to the voice of Sarai. Sarai, Abram's wife, took Hagar the Egyptian, her servant, after Abram had lived ten years in the land of Canaan, and gave her to Abram her husband to be his wife. He went in to Hagar, and she conceived. When she saw that she had conceived, her mistress was despised in her eyes. Sarai said to Abram, 'This wrong is your fault. I gave my servant into your bosom, and when she saw that she had conceived, she despised me. May Yahweh judge between me and you.' But Abram said to Sarai, 'Behold, your maid is in your hand. Do to her whatever is good in your eyes.' Sarai dealt harshly with her, and she fled from her face." By this time, the Bible tells us in Genesis 16:16 that Abram was now eighty-six years old, which would have made Sarai in her late seventies. And still, they had no son.

There are obviously quite a few lessons to be learned from this story. For starters, why did Hagar despise Sarai? Could it have been because in that culture, it was considered a curse from God for a woman to be unable to bear children? Did Hagar consider her mistress to be "less of a woman" because she could not have children? Was it because, as a servant, Hagar had no say in what Sarai and Abram did to her, and perhaps this sexual encounter between Hagar and Abram was not consensual on Hagar's part? Maybe Hagar thought that if Sarai had been able to get pregnant herself, Hagar would not have been forced to sleep with her master. Maybe Hagar was upset that she was going to have to endure a nine-month pregnancy and then not even get to keep her own child afterward. That alone could have caused hard feelings between these two women, and I imagine that there was quite a bit of strife in this household because of these circumstances, don't you? And of course, notice how Sarai is the one who instigated the entire situation, using her maidservant Hagar to have a child with Abram and then turning around and blaming all the resulting conflict on her husband Abram. Whatever the reason, Sarai's impulsivity led to hostility not only between her and her maidservant but between Sarai and her husband Abram, too. I'll bet poor Abram had just about decided at that point that he couldn't win with these two women in his household!

On the other hand, as a woman who has struggled with infertility herself, I honestly can understand how poor Sarah must have felt. Wanting a child. Having been promised a child by God, but waiting. Waiting. Feeling like life is passing you by. Listening to the ticking of your biological clock and knowing that with every year that passes, the chances of your conceiving a child are dwindling. Seeing your friends and peers celebrating motherhood and yet you are still waiting. In your heart, you know as you continue to age that it will take a miracle for you to realize the fulfillment of your dreams. But you have never seen a miracle in your lifetime. You don't even know of anyone who has. Why should God bless you, of all people, with a miracle? What makes you so special? And yet you continue to wait. And suffer in silence.

Isn't it tempting for us to react just like Sarai when we pray for something and then we must wait an agonizingly long time for an answer from God? Even being asked to wait beyond the point of logic? Don't we sometimes just want to take the entire situation into our own hands and force the events to work out the way in which we want them? Because we can't see otherwise how what was promised will ever happen. Trying to force a situation to turn out the way we want is never advisable because God can see all the minute details that we cannot. He can see our future, and He knows infinitely better what we need and when we need it. But Sarah was human, and let's face it, we humans are not noted for our patience.

By making them wait, God was testing the faith of Abram and Sarai. After all, face it, with each passing year, they weren't getting any younger, and soon, they were past the logical ages of childbearing. As the years passed and they continued to grow older, I'm sure that Abram and Sarai began to think that God had forgotten His promise to them. And yet in Genesis 17:1–8, God reiterated His covenant with Abram and even changed his name to Abraham, meaning "father of many." By delaying His answer, God was showing Abraham and Sarah that they were going to have to rely on God's power for the fulfillment of His promise to them. Still as the years passed, it must have seemed almost cruel to prolong this promise when Sarah and Abraham couldn't see any possibility of it coming to pass. I feel sure that there must have been days when this couple struggled with their faith.

In Genesis 17:15–21, we read, "God said to Abraham, 'As for Sarai your wife, you shall not call her name Sarai, but her name will be Sarah. I will bless her, and moreover I will give you a son by her. Yes, I will bless her, and she will be a mother of nations. Kings of peoples will come from her.' Then Abraham fell on his face, and laughed, and said in his heart, 'Will a child be born to him who is one hundred years old? Will Sarah, who is ninety years old, give birth?' Abraham said to God, 'Oh, that Ishmael might live before you!' God said, 'No, but Sarah, your wife, will bear you a son. You shall call his name Isaac. I will establish my covenant with him, for an everlasting covenant for his offspring after him. As for Ishmael, I have heard you. Behold, I have blessed him, and will make him fruitful, and will multiply him exceedingly. He will become the father of twelve princes, and I will make him a great nation. But I will establish my covenant with Isaac, whom Sarah will bear to you at this set time next year.'"

Suddenly, the promise of God was not some vague in-the-distant-future pledge, but a specific "it will happen when I say so" oath. Can you imagine the delight of both Sarah and Abraham when they realized that God was finally going to fulfill His promise to them?

Genesis 21:1–2 tells us that Sarah had a son, Isaac, at the exact time that God had told her that she would. Can you imagine their elation? Their sense of wonderment. But as a woman, part of me wonders how Sarah felt knowing that because she was so old when she had Isaac, she might not live to see him grow to adulthood. That too had to be painful for her to bear.

As I stated before, when my husband and I tried to adopt baby Maggie, she was our fourth attempt at adoption. Our previous three attempts had resulted in failure, and our third attempt was terminated by the adoption agency, who had decided that my husband, Rick, would be "too old by the time our baby would be old enough to graduate from high school." (Several foreign countries have age requirements for international adoptions, and Rick and I were pushing the limits.)

But when we brought Maggie home from the NICU, she was two months old. At that time, Rick was fifty-one years old and I was forty-four. We used to laugh about what a good baby Maggie was because she would always go to sleep at 10:00 p.m. and sleep through the night until six thirty the next morning. Our joke was that because we were "so old" when we finally brought a baby home, God knew that we needed a good one! I have often wondered if Isaac was a good baby too for Abraham and Sarah.

The New Testament points out how God kept His Word to Abraham even though Abraham had to wait years for the fulfillment of the promise made by God. In Hebrews 6:13–15, we read, "For when God made a promise to Abraham, since he could swear by no one greater, he swore by himself, saying, 'Surely blessing I will bless you, and multiplying I will multiply you.' Thus, having patiently endured, he obtained the promise."

Waiting for anything we really want is difficult at best and nearly impossible at worst. Society doesn't help with its fast pace and tendency to push us all to want immediate gratification. Instant connection to others via FaceTime, text messages, Instagram, and phone calls. Buy it by charging it on your credit card now and worry about paying for it later. Do you know which button is pushed more frequently than any other on an elevator? The "door close" button because we are all so impatient to be on our way.

In 1 Samuel 13, we read of another person who got into trouble by not waiting on God. Verses 5–14 of this chapter say, "The Philistines assembled themselves together to fight with Israel, thirty thousand chariots, and six thousand horsemen, and people as the sand which is on the seashore in multitude. They came up and encamped in Michmash, eastward of Beth Aven. When the men of Israel saw that they were in trouble (for the people were distressed), then the people hid themselves in caves, in thickets, in rocks, in tombs and in pits. Now some of the Hebrews had gone over the Jordan to the land of Gad and Gilead; but as for Saul, he was yet in Gilgal, and all the people followed him trembling. He stayed seven days, according to the time set by Samuel, but Samuel didn't come to Gilgal, and the people were scattering from him. Saul said, 'Bring the burnt offering to me here, and the peace offerings.' He offered the burnt offering. It came to pass that as soon as he had finished offering the burnt offering, behold, Samuel came; and Saul went out to meet him, that he might greet him. Samuel said, 'What have you done?' Saul said, 'Because I saw that the people were scattering from me, and that you didn't come within the days appointed, and that the Philistines assembled themselves together at Michmash; therefore I said, "Now the Philistines will come down on me to Gilgal, and I haven't entreated the favor of Yahweh." I forced myself therefore, and offered the burnt offering.' Samuel said to Saul, 'You have done foolishly. You have not kept the commandment of Yahweh your God, which he commanded you; for now Yahweh would have established your kingdom on Israel forever. But now your kingdom will not continue. Yahweh has sought for himself a man after his own heart, and Yahweh has appointed him to be prince over his people, because you have not kept that which Yahweh commanded you.'"

Saul knew that he needed to ask for God's blessing before going into battle against the Philistines. He knew that the prophet Samuel was the actual person who was supposed to offer the burnt sacrifice, but when Samuel didn't show up at the appointed time, Saul decided to do what he was forbidden to do by Mosaic law. As a result, he lost his kingship over Israel. God rejected Saul for another man He had selected Himself: David. Was it worth it to Saul to be impulsive and not wait to do things God's way? Not hardly. Do you think that he, like Sarah, came to regret his actions? Probably.

In 2 Chronicles 16:7–13, we read of another person who did not wait for the Lord. These verses say, "At that time Hanani the seer came to Asa king of Judah, and said to him, 'Because you have relied on the king of Syria, and have not relied on Yahweh your God, therefore the army of the king of Syria has escaped out of your hand. Weren't the Ethiopians and the Lubim a huge army, with chariots and exceedingly many horsemen? Yet, because you relied on Yahweh, he delivered them into your hand. For Yahweh's eyes rush back and forth throughout the whole earth, to show himself strong in the behalf of them whose heart is perfect toward him. You have done foolishly in this: for from now on you will have wars.' Then Asa was angry with the seer, and put him in the prison; for he was in a rage with him because of this thing. Asa oppressed some of the people at the same time. Behold, the acts of Asa, first and last, behold, they are written in the book of the kings of Judah and Israel. In the thirty-ninth year of his reign, Asa was diseased in his feet. His disease was exceedingly great; yet in his disease he did not seek Yahweh, but just the physicians. Asa slept with his fathers and died in the forty-first year of his reign." Because of trying to do things his own way, King Asa lost peace, his kingship, and his health.

How many times, for example, do teenagers try to force a relationship they are currently in to the next stage, believing perhaps that they are in love with the person they are dating when they haven't lived long enough to understand what true love entails? How many times, as adults, do we do the same thing trying to force things to work out the way we want when it comes to the job we really want or that new home or the chance to move across the country?

Have you ever wanted something to happen so badly in your life that you lost your perspective? Unfortunately, it's easy to do, and those of us who tend to lead with our emotions must guard against this.

My mother told me of the time that she and my father put in a bid on the house that I grew up in, and before they had even closed the deal on that house, my father would drive over and mow that yard because he wanted that house so badly! They hadn't even been approved for the loan, but my dad was willing to spend some of his precious time mowing grass at a house that they might not even have gotten! Fortunately, they did get the house, but my mother admitted to being put off by my father's impulsivity and, as she called it, "unreasonableness."

Are there things we can focus on while we wait for God's answers to our prayers? Are there scriptures that can help us control our impatience and trust God's timing?

The first part of verse 1 of Psalm 37 (NIV) says, "Be still before the Lord and wait patiently for him." The psalmist knew the importance of patience when waiting on the Lord for his answers to prayers. Becoming impatient does not show Christian maturity.

Psalm 130:5 says, "I wait for Yahweh. My soul waits. I hope in his word." God's Word can teach us patience, and while we are waiting for God's reply, it is beneficial to dig deeply into scripture and immerse yourself in the promises of God. What better way to take your mind off the wait than to learn more about your heavenly Father who loves you and only wants what is best for you?

Psalm 106:6–15 says, "We have sinned with our fathers. We have committed iniquity. We have done wickedly. Our fathers didn't understand your wonders in Egypt. They didn't remember the multitude of your loving kindnesses, but were rebellious at the sea, even at the Red Sea. Nevertheless, he saved them for his name's sake, that he might make his mighty power known. He rebuked the Red Sea also, and it was dried up, so he led them through the depths, as through a desert. He saved them from the hand of him who hated them, and redeemed them from the hand of the enemy. The waters covered their adversaries. There was not one of them left. Then they believed his words. They sang his praise. They soon forgot his works. *They didn't wait for his counsel,* but gave in to craving in the desert, and tested God in the wasteland. *He gave them their request, but sent leanness into their soul"* (emphasis mine).

Did you notice those two passages I emphasized in the Bible verses above? "They didn't wait for his counsel" and "He gave them their request"? Remember how the Israelites kept grumbling and complaining in the desert? This passage teaches us that if you complain enough, God may give you exactly what you think you want even if it's not what's best for you or even if it's not what He has planned for you. Notice also in the second emphasized passage above: "He gave them their request, but sent leanness into their soul." Did God's giving the Israelites what they thought they wanted to deepen their faith and trust in Him? No. The words "He sent leanness into their soul" means that what He gave them was not the deep blessing He had intended. Isn't it sad that God wanted to richly bless the Israelites, but they were willing to settle for second or even third best because they grew impatient with God?

The prophet Micah in Micah 7:7 says, "Therefore I will look to the Lord; I will wait for the God of my salvation; My God will hear me." While you are waiting for God's answer, don't allow the devil to convince you that God does not hear your prayers or that God really doesn't care about you. The Bible teaches us over and over that God does hear and that He does care for each of us.

God truly wants what is best for us (even if we don't always understand His methods or His reasoning), but one of the most important lessons we must learn in developing a deeper faith in Him is to wait for His timing. Having to wait is almost always a test of our faith. Only by waiting and trusting can we pass this test. Waiting for God is never a waste of time! There are lessons to be learned during our periods of waiting, and we need to focus on what God is teaching us. Waiting on God can deepen our faith and increase our trust in Him.

Habakkuk 2:1 says, "I will stand at my watch and station myself on the ramparts. I will look to see what he will say to me, and what I am to give to this complaint." The entire book of Habakkuk is about the prophet waiting for God to take care of evildoers and injustice—in His own timing. If you have time this week, read this oft-overlooked gem in the Old Testament. This little book focuses on moving from doubt regarding what God is doing to absolute trust in Him to accomplish His purpose by whatever means.

Some people think that Judas Iscariot believed that Jesus intended to set up an earthly kingdom, and by betraying Jesus to the chief priests, Judas was trying to force Jesus to establish His kingdom earlier than anticipated. *If* Judas *was* trying to force along the events in Jerusalem, he failed, because Jesus had proposed His kingdom to be a spiritual one all along, and Judas merely played into God's plan of salvation.

In the New Testament, the Lord's half brother, James, writes in his epistle, James 1:2–4, "Consider it pure joy, my brothers, whenever you face trials of many kinds, because you know that the testing of your faith develops perseverance. Perseverance must finish its work so that you may be mature and complete, not lacking anything." One of the Christian's duties is to learn patience "by the testing of your faith." The writer, James, says that patience helps us become mature Christians.

Maybe God makes us wait for His answers to our prayers to allow us time to see if what we *think* we want is what we really want or to give us a deeper appreciation for His response when it finally does come, or even to give us time to mature and thus be ready to use His gift to us more wisely. How long will we persevere when we think we want something? One day? Two? If it's important to us, will we keep praying and praying until we get an answer from God? How determined are we? Determined enough to hang in there or wavering in what we think we want?

Waiting for God to act in our lives requires tremendous faith, courage, strength, and patience. There are lessons that can only be learned when we are listening to God's voice. By trying to rush circumstances along according to our timetable, we miss out on the lessons God has planned for us to learn. Forcing situations to work out the way we want can eliminate what God is trying to teach us.

In the next chapter, we will study some things we can do while we are waiting for God to answer our prayers.

THOUGHT QUESTIONS

1. Have you ever desperately wanted something to happen in your life and found yourself becoming impatient while waiting for it to come to fruition? What was it, if you don't mind sharing?

2. Have you ever tried to force a situation to work out the way you wanted because you were tired of waiting for it to work out on its own in God's timing? How did that work out for you? What were the consequences of your forcing the situation? Do you wish now that you would have waited for it to have all come to pass naturally without your forcing the situation? Why or why not?

3. Do you think it is a sin to grow impatient with God? Why or why not?

4. Do you believe that the motivation for Judas Iscariot's actions was to force the hand of Jesus into establishing His earthly kingdom sooner than planned? If not, what do you think Judas's motives were for betraying Jesus?

5. What are some things that might be difficult for us to submit to God's will?

LESSON 13

While We Wait

WHILE WE ARE WAITING FOR GOD TO ANSWER OUR PRAYERS, WHAT CAN we be doing in the meantime?

First, we can continue to pray. In Acts 1:4, the apostles are told to wait in Jerusalem for the coming of the Holy Spirit. They were not to begin their ministry. They were not to return to their fishing or previous occupations. They were to go to Jerusalem and wait.

Verses 12–14 of this same chapter say, "Then they returned to Jerusalem from the hill called the Mount of Olives, a Sabbath's day walk from the city. When they arrived, they went upstairs to the room where they were staying. Those present were Peter, John, James and Andrew, Phillip and Thomas, Bartholomew and Matthew, James son of Alphaeus and Simon the Zealot, and Judas son of James. They all joined together constantly in prayer, along with the women and Mary the mother of Jesus and with his brothers." Why were they praying? Not for the coming of the Holy Spirit because He had already been promised to them. More than likely, they were praying for their future evangelistic efforts and for strength and courage for one another in the midst of opposition to the Gospel. Think of it, this was the first prayer meeting of the church! While they were waiting in Jerusalem, the disciples were not idle. While they waited, they prayed. We too should pray while we wait for an answer from God.

We can learn persistence from the Canaanite woman in Matthew 15:21–28 or from the woman Jesus described in His parable in Luke 18:1–8. Neither of them intended to take no for an answer! We too should keep praying for what we want. Persistence is what these two women embodied, and persistence is what we need to exhibit while waiting for God to answer our prayers.

There are also Bible verses that we can meditate on while we are waiting for God to answer our prayers.

Psalm 46:10 says, "Be still, and know that I am God." Ponder what this verse is saying to you. Be still. Stop worrying. Stop struggling. Stop striving. Be still and *know* that "I am God." This isn't a guess. It isn't a fallacy. It is an established fact! "Know that I am God!" What else do you need to know? He is God, the Creator of the world, of time, of life, of salvation. He's got this! Whatever you are fretting about, whatever worries you, whatever circumstance you find yourself in, God is in control. Read that again: *God is in control*, not Satan, not your emotions, not other humans, and not even your circumstances. God is in control of everything. What a comforting thought. Our heavenly Father who loves each and every one of us is in control of this crazy, sin-filled world that we live in, and He has plans for you and me.

When this world seems to be spiraling out of control, remember two things: it was God who put the king in power over Egypt in the first place (see Exodus 1:8–10), and when the plaques from God hit the land of Egypt, the Israelite nation and their livestock were spared (see Exodus 8:21–24; 9:1–7; 9:13–26; 10:21–23; and 11:4–7).

An oft-quoted passage in Romans 8:28 says, "We know that all things work together for good for those who love God, who are called according to his purpose." This verse doesn't say that everything that happens to us will be good, but that God *will work it out* for our good. Struggles make us stronger. Trials teach us patience. Suffering molds us into the kind of people God wants us to be. And did you catch that, "*all things* work together for good …"? God has a plan for everything that happens in our lives. Everything. Nothing happens to us that God cannot use for His divine purpose.

The Bible even teaches us that God uses the wicked for His purposes. Proverbs 16:4 tells us, "Yahweh has made everything for its own end—yes, even the wicked for the day of evil." Throughout the Bible, we learn that God used ungodly nations like Assyria and Babylon to punish Israel and Judah for their disobedience.

Matthew 10:29 tells us, "Aren't two sparrows sold for an assarion coin? Not one of them falls on the ground apart from your Father's will." God even knows when a little bird falls to the ground. How much more aware is He of what you are going through!

Do you know why the writer of Proverbs 5:5 says, "Trust in Yahweh with all your heart, and don't lean on your own understanding"? We think we are wise. Sometimes in our arrogance, we think we know more than God. But God is infinitely wiser than all of us. He sees circumstances now, and in our futures, and He knows what is best for us. That is why we should trust God.

Other scriptures to meditate upon while waiting for God's answers to your prayers include Ecclesiastes 3:1; Psalm 27:14; 31:14–15; 37:7–8; and 40:1.

Even the demons acknowledge that God works according to His own timetable. Matthew 8:28–29 tells us, "When he arrived at the other side in the region of the Gadarenes, two demon-possessed men coming from the tombs met him. They were so violent that no one could pass that way. 'What do you want with us, Son of God?' they shouted. 'Have you come to torture us before the appointed time?'" Even the demons acknowledged that God had a specific time when He planned to send His Son into the world to save His people. He also had a specific time when Jesus was to begin His ministry.

Romans 5:6 also tells us, "You see, at just the right time, when we were still powerless, Christ died for the ungodly."

Paul reiterates this thought in Galatians 4:4, which says, "But when the time had fully come, God sent his Son, born of a woman, born under law."

The entire Old Testament foretold of the coming of the Messiah, the one who would save the world. Then God was silent for 400 years between the end of the Old Testament and the New Testament. But when the time was right, God sent His Son into the world to be born of a virgin. Everything God does or allows to happen has a time and a purpose.

First Peter 5:6 says, "Humble yourselves, therefore, under God's mighty hand, that he may lift you up in due time." That is a promise. In due time, His time, God will lift each of us up if we humble ourselves under His mighty hand and submit to His will and His timing.

As was pointed out in a previous chapter, 2 Peter 3:8 reads as follows: "But don't forget this one thing, beloved, that one day is with the Lord as a thousand years, and a thousand years as one day." We must remember that God is not bound by time like we are. Time has no meaning for God. He lives in the present all the time. One day, we too will only live in the present for eternity. There will be no past. No future. Just one glorious day with the Lord.

While we are waiting, we need to focus on passages such as Romans 8:18–25, which says, "For I consider that the sufferings of this present time are not worthy to be compared with the glory that will be revealed toward us. For the creation waits with eager expectation for the children of God to be revealed. For the creation was subjected to vanity, not of its own will, but because of him who subjected it, in hope that the creation itself also will be delivered from the bondage of decay into the liberty of the glory of the children of God. For we know that the whole creation groans and travails in pain together until now. Not only so, but ourselves also, who have the first fruits of the spirit, even we ourselves groan within ourselves, waiting for adoption, the redemption of our body. For we were saved in hope, but hope that is seen is not hope. For who hopes for that which he sees? But if we hope for that which we don't see, we wait for it with patience."

Unfortunately, our world is a fast-paced one, and having to wait for anything to happen is not an easy thing to do.

Why does God make us wait? To test our patience perhaps. To test our faith. To allow us time to see if what we think we want is what we really want. To give us a deeper appreciation for His response when He finally does answer our prayers. Or perhaps to give us a chance to grow and mature and thus be ready to use His gift of an answer more wisely when it does come to pass. There are lessons that can only be learned while we are waiting for God's timing. By trying to rush circumstances according to our own timetables, we miss out on the lessons God had in mind for us to learn.

James, the Lord's half brother, tells us in James 5:7–8, "Be patient therefore, brothers, until the coming of the Lord. Behold, the farmer waits for the precious fruit of the earth, being patient over it, until it receives the early and late rain. You also be patient. Establish your hearts, for the coming of the Lord is at hand." What does a farmer do when it's wintertime and they are not planting, weeding, or harvesting their crops? Anyone who has ever worked on a farm knows that work continues year-round. They might be planting, growing, and harvesting winter crops such as kale, onions, leeks, etc. They might be planning and preparing their fields for their springtime planting. They might be working on farm equipment, performing maintenance tasks, taking care of livestock, and learning new farming techniques. The point of all this is simply that while they are waiting for spring, farmers keep busy. There is always work to be done around a farm, just as there is always work to be done in the Lord's kingdom. Keeping busy is a great antidote to boredom, anxiety, and impatience.

Acts 9:1–19 tells the story of the great apostle, Paul, who was blinded on the road to Damascus by the Lord. Verse 9 says, "He was without sight for three days, and neither ate nor drank." Verse 11 of this same passage says that the Lord said to Ananias, "Arise and go to the street which is called Straight, and inquire in the house of Judah for one named Saul, a man of Tarsus. For behold, he is praying." After being blinded, what did Saul do for three days? This passage teaches us that he prayed and fasted. How many times do we think to pray and fast when we are awaiting God's answer to our prayers? Doing so might show God the sincerity of our hearts.

All of us who believe in and obey the Lord Jesus Christ are waiting for the promise of heaven, and although it may be in the near future for some of us, or in the distant future, we cling to the hope of that promise. And while waiting and hoping, we must continue to work and obey the Lord.

Hebrews 12:1–3 is a beautiful passage and one of my personal favorites. It tells us what we need to do as we wait for our heavenly reward. "Therefore let's also, seeing we are surrounded by so great a cloud of witnesses, lay aside every weight and the sin which so easily entangles us, and let's run with perseverance the race that is set before us, looking to Jesus, the author and perfector of faith, who for the joy that was set before him endured the cross, despising its shame, and has sat down at the right hand of the throne of God. For consider him who has endured such contradiction of sinners against himself, that you do not grow weary, fainting in your souls." What are the *weights* that the apostle Paul mentions in this passage? Could they be our expectations, our hang-ups, our past, basically anything that weighs us down and keeps us from running the race? But as many of us know, at least those of us who have lived several decades, the "race" Paul describes is not a sprint, but a race of endurance.

My sister and I were both distance runners in high school and college. Neither of us had the speed for sprints, but we both had the endurance and stamina for distance running. Sprints are all about simply running a short distance as fast as possible. These are mostly physical races. Distance running is more of a mental challenge, pacing oneself, not using up too much energy at the beginning of the race, and not saving too much for the end. It's also all about keeping up with the lead runner so as not to lose too much of a head start and not fall too far behind. It's about keeping your focus and your pace consistently.

Philippians 3:12–14 remind us, "Not that I have already obtained, or am already made perfect, but I press on, that I may take hold of that for which also I was taken hold of by Christ Jesus. Brothers, I do not regard myself as yet having taken hold, but one thing I do: forgetting the things which are behind, and stretching forward to the things which are before, I press on toward the goal for the prize of the high calling of God in Christ Jesus."

While we are waiting for God's answers to our prayers, we especially need to focus on one of the most beloved and comforting passages in the Bible. No wonder it is used at so many funerals because the promise in it is uplifting and consolatory! It is found in the Gospel of John 14:1–3, and it says, "Do not let your hearts be troubled. Believe in God. Believe also in me. In my Father's house are many homes. If it weren't so, I would have told you. I am going to prepare a place for you. If I go and prepare a place for you, I will come again, and will receive you to myself, that where I am, you may be there also."

While we are awaiting a response from God to our prayers, we need to remember that God is waiting too. Second Peter 3:9 tells us, "The Lord is not slow concerning his promise, as some count slowness: but he is patient with us, not wishing that anyone should perish, but that all should come to repentance." God is waiting for all to come to Him, believing that He is the Creator and Lord and Savior of all.

Something that would help all of us while we are waiting for an answer from God in response to a prayer request of ours would be to focus on how much He has already blessed us! The prophet Isaiah says in Isaiah 12:4–5, "In that day you will say, 'Give thanks to Yahweh! Call on his name. Declare his doings among the peoples. Proclaim that his name is exalted. Sing to Yahweh, for he has done excellent things! Let this be known in all the earth.'" Do we really take the time to focus on how really blessed we are, or do we only think of those things we don't have? One of our greatest blessings is our ability to count our blessings! And the ability to pray to God is one of our biggest blessings of all!

THOUGHT QUESTIONS

1. What advice would you give others who are waiting for God's response to their prayers?

2. What can you do while waiting for an answer to your prayers?

3. Why do you think God makes us wait for His answer to our prayers? What is the purpose of our waiting?

4. Do you know of someone who is so laid-back that waiting never seems to make them impatient? What can you learn from this person?

ABOUT THE AUTHOR

 JOYCE CHURCH BRUNO grew up in a small West Virginia town situated on the banks of the beautiful Ohio River. Now she lives in Centerville, TN with Rick, her husband of almost 34 years and their three cats. She is a registered nurse who fills in at the emergency department, endoscopy clinic and medical rehab unit of the local hospital. She is also a member of the Fairfield church of Christ.

Joyce has been writing since she was a teenager, but this is her first published book. She is already hard at work on her second writing project.

Printed in the United States
by Baker & Taylor Publisher Services